HAUNTED NEWCASTLE

HAUNTED NEWCASTLE

DARREN W. RITSON

FOREWORD BY ALAN MURDIE

The History Press

This book is dedicated to my mother and father, Jean and Walter; to my brother, Gary; and to my girls – Jayne and Abbey.

Frontispiece: *The Holy Jesus Hospital on City Road is said to be one of two surviving seventeenth-century buildings in Newcastle. Behind the building stands a fourteenth-century Augustinian tower.*

First published 2009

The History Press
The Mill, Brimscombe Port
Stroud, Gloucestershire, GL5 2QG
www.thehistorypress.co.uk

Reprinted 2009, 2012, 2013

British Library Cataloguing in Publication Data.
A catalogue record for this book is available from the British Library.

ISBN 978 0 7524 4880 0

Typesetting and origination by The History Press

CONTENTS

Also by the Author

The South Shields Poltergeist: One Family's Fight Against an Invisible Intruder (with Michael J. Hallowell)

Haunted Durham

Ghosts at Christmas

Haunted Berwick

Haunted Northumberland

The Haunting of Willington Mill: The Truth Behind England's Most Enigmatic Ghost Story (with Michael J. Hallowell)

Haunted Tyneside

Haunted Carlisle

Haunted Wearside

FOREWORD

The author of any regionally orientated ghost book such as *Haunted Newcastle* faces the difficult task of satisfying at least three distinct audiences. Firstly, there is a large group of people who want to be simply entertained by a thrilling ghost story, suitable for telling at Christmas time or reading alone in the comfort and security of one's home with the lights dimmed. Secondly, there is a smaller – but no less demanding – audience who see the paranormal as a serious matter for study and debate, and view it as providing insights upon fundamental questions regarding the nature of existence and the possibility of life after death. And there is a third and perhaps growing audience, those who live in, and know the area concerned and who want a handbook to use to go and directly investigate haunted sites. On opening a regional ghost book they will soon be eagerly searching for details of ghosts in local buildings which they know and frequent, with every intention of making a personal visit in the very hope of experiencing paranormal activity themselves.

Whichever of these categories the reader may fall into – and in many cases they overlap – I am sure that Darren Ritson's book will be appreciated and enjoyed by many. Perhaps only pure thrill-seekers may be a touch disappointed to find that genuine ghosts seldom resemble the dramatic phantoms of supernatural fiction (although I suspect many researchers might quit the field if they did!). But the accounts in this book are none the less fascinating for this, and whatever view the reader takes of reports of ghosts and ghostly phenomena, I am certain this is a book which will be of great value to anyone with a serious interest in Tyneside hauntings.

A book such as *Haunted Newcastle* is also long overdue. For myself, with a family background partly from the Newcastle area, I have long held an interest in ghost reports emanating from the city and its environs. However, I have hitherto been rather disappointed to find relatively few first-hand reports of apparitions and haunting events in published works. Even in the heyday of spontaneous case collecting in the early years of the Society for Psychical Research, relatively little material was gathered in and around Newcastle. The society zealously pursued cases of both crisis apparitions of persons seen at the point of death (published in the monumental *Phantasms of the Living* (1886)) and more standard accounts of haunted houses, but few cases seemed to have been gathered on Tyneside. Even over a century later – in marked contrast to the celebrated ghosts of other cities such as London, York, Derby and Edinburgh – the phantoms receive little publicity. As the author remarks, the city was very much virgin

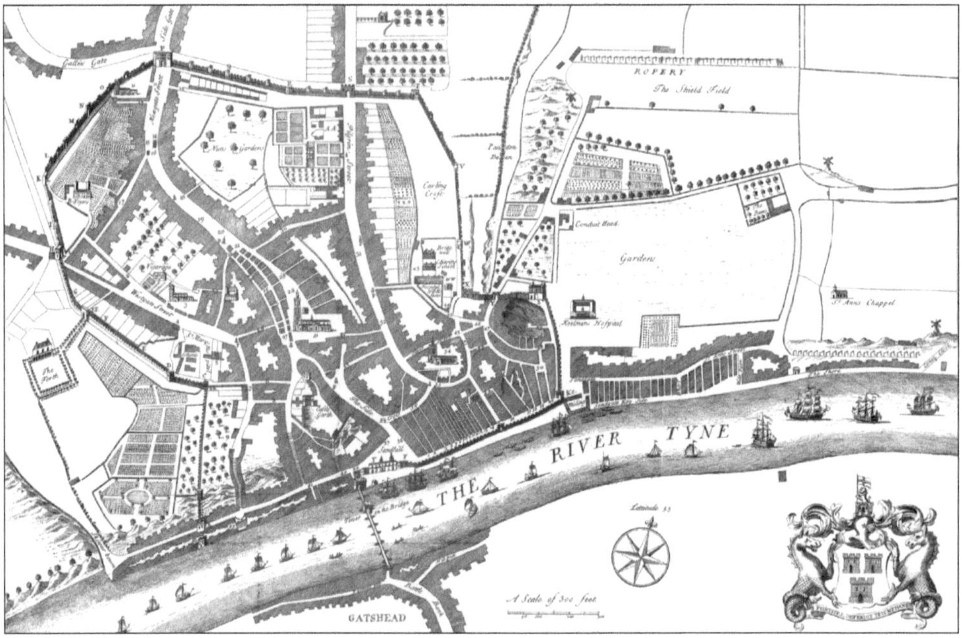

A Bourne Map of Newcastle upon Tyne from 1736 showing the full route of the city walls. (Courtesy of Newcastle Libraries and Information Service)

territory in terms of books and published reports of apparitions and ghostly activity when he began collecting the material contained herein.

For those engaged in psychical research this seeming absence of material may also be rather surprising. If there is any truth in the view that psychic phenomena may be linked with the presence of water, Newcastle upon Tyne might well be expected to have many accounts of noisy hauntings, even spurious ones caused by the effects of tides and underground water channels. This theory – which was popular with certain psychic researchers during the 1950s and '60s as an explanation for poltergeist phenomena and anomalous sounds such as footsteps, knocks and groans – is now largely discredited. Similarly, proponents of the more esoteric theory of 'window areas' – that there are certain places particularly prone to ghostly and psychic occurrences – might conclude that Newcastle is not one of them.

However, absence of evidence is not evidence of absence, and I think that other factors have been at work and have kept Newcastle ghost experiences a predominantly local affair. A strong sense of regional identity and local patriotism for which the area is justly famous has been an influence. As Darren Ritson has discovered, local people have an endless number of stories of ghostly experiences, but have largely kept them local and to themselves – as is their privilege. It has thus required determined local researchers to tap into this rich source of oral tradition and record it. As a local born and bred, Darren Ritson has been ideally placed to engage with local people and receive their testimony, and this book is a tribute to his labours. The harvest has been great and regrettably space does not allow for inclusion of all the accounts and data which have been gathered. Attractive as theories of 'most haunted cities' and 'window areas' may be, books like this one lead me to believe they are really no more than statistical effects, which ultimately reflect the dedication and commitment of individual researchers. *Haunted Newcastle* demonstrates what I have come to believe about all areas of the UK, and indeed the rest of world. Every related society of which we have a record has had a belief in ghosts and the return of the dead in one form or another. Accounts of haunting phenomena are to be found everywhere, if you are prepared to go and look. What is necessary are dedicated people prepared to collect testimony – and in this regard, Darren Ritson has done a very good job.

The volume of material gathered in this collection is also owed much to the fact that the author is no mere armchair or internet-surfing ghost hunter, but one of the variety who actually goes out and looks. He has visited many reputedly haunted sites and investigated numerous cases personally. Despite the view propagated by certain parts of the mass media (particularly on some very dubious television shows) that ghost hunting is a thrilling activity filled with unexplained events at every turn, the reverse is more usually the case. As another former chairman of the Ghost Club, Tom Perrot, once wisely said to me, 'All too frequently my ghost hunting equipment consists of a pencil, a notebook and a sympathetic ear.' Proper investigation requires not simply a night-time vigil but a great deal of follow-up work. This often involves laborious trawls through official records, libraries and archives, as well as contacting a wide range of individuals and agencies who may hold key information about a particular site.

Newcastle in 1600. (Courtesy of Newcastle Libraries and Information Service)

To investigate an alleged haunting properly can take weeks, if not months of effort. At the early stages there is often little beyond the account of a puzzled or frightened witness to go on. Proper research can demand the gathering and examination of a great deal of diverse evidence. It is rare that investigators get to have experiences of an apparent ghost, although Darren Ritson has had some measure of success at certain sites. More often than not these efforts result in more unresolved questions than one began with.

Fortunately, the whole topic of ghosts is today increasingly receiving more academic and informed attention than for many years. This interest on the part of academia is long overdue. Reports of ghosts – whatever one may believe about them – are increasingly being studied and examined by scholars from a wide range of disciplines, including psychologists, physicists, historians and folklorists. Increasingly, it is recognised that ghost encounters can shed light on many aspects of human experience, whatever the ultimate nature of the phenomena may be. Parapsychologists – of whom the UK has a growing number – are also taking up with renewed interest the issue of so-called 'spontaneous cases'; in other words, those types of psychic phenomena occurring outside the laboratory and which are experienced by the population at large. Whilst these are welcome developments, we must never forget the crucial work which researchers such as Darren Ritson perform in gathering fresh data at source. Books such as *Haunted Newcastle* lay a pioneering path for researchers delving into the vast territory of the unexplained, and the publication of this volume is warmly welcomed as a further informed contribution to the field. And I am also sure that this will be a book that many will read for pleasure for many years to come.

Alan Murdie
Head of the Spontaneous Cases Committee
for the Society for Psychical Research,
and former chairman of the Ghost Club

ACKNOWLEDGEMENTS

Alan Murdie (Head of the Spontaneous Cases Committee for the Society for Psychical Research, and former chairman of the Ghost Club) for his help and kindness and for agreeing to pen the Foreword to this book. My acquaintances at the Society for Psychical Research who have given me so much real support and encouragement during my research these last few years. The Ghost Club of Great Britain for its support, and encouragement. My father, Walter Ritson, for supplying me with many photographs from his archives for inclusion in this book. Mike Hallowell for his endless help and encouragement. To Jon Downes from the Centre for Fortean Zoology (CFZ) – the world's largest mystery animal research group. The members of the North East Ghost Research Team and G.H.O.S.T. for helping with the investigations contained herein. Julie Olley for the wonderful illustrations contained throughout the book. Suzanne Hitchinson (*née* McKay) and Sam Fox for inviting me to their investigation at the Fusilier public house. The various correspondents and witnesses that have sent me material to use in this book – without their letters these ghost stories may never have been told. Paul McDonald at Newcastle Keep for his help and assistance. Trevor Brown for the use of his rather odd 'mist photo' and his explanation as to how it came to be photographed. Steve Taylor from the Newcastle Ghost Walk and Alone in the Dark Entertainment for various stories relayed. To everyone that has taken time out to talk to me and share their experiences during my research and compilation of this book, including pub landlords, property owners, historians, museum guides, shop assistants, factory workers, students and everyone else. Many thanks must also go to the Newcastle Libraries and Information Service for allowing me to reproduce some of their pictures. To Gladys Parker and all the volunteers at Byker Community Centre, Jo Bean and the staff at El-Coto restaurant, the owners of the Coroner's Court, the staff and wardens at Newcastle Keep, to Gemma Gorner, Liz Mills, Jo Risolino – and of course 'Tom' – and to Lee and Kelly from the Fusilier public house for allowing overnight access to their premises for our investigations. Special thanks go to Cate Ludlow and the staff at The History Press for having faith in me – working with you on this book has been an absolute pleasure. All photographs taken by Darren W. Ritson unless otherwise stated.

Other books by Darren W. Ritson include: *The South Shields Poltergeist – One Family's Fight against an Invisible Intruder* (with Michael J. Hallowell. Published by The History Press, 2008).

SOME THOUGHTS ON NEWCASTLE

Newcastle is a noble town tho' in a bottom, it most resembles London of any place in England, its buildings are lofty and large of brick mostly or stone; the streetes are very broad and handsome and very well pitch'd and many of them with very fine conduits of water in each, always running into a large stone Cistern for every bodyes use. Their shops are good and are of distinct trades. Saturday is the biggest market day and the market is like a faire for all sorts of provision and goods are very cheape.

Celia Fiennes – 1698

Newcastle is spacious, extended, infinitely populous place; tis seated upon the river Tyne, which is here a noble, large and deep river, and ships of any reasonable burthen may come safely up to the very town. As the town lies on both sides of the river, the parts are join'd by a very strong and stately stone bridge of seven arches rather larger than the arches of London Bridge; and the bridge is built into a street of houses also, as is London Bridge. They built ships here to perfection, I mean as to strength, and firmness, and to bear the sea; and as the coal trade occasions a great demand for such strong ships, a great many are built here.

Daniel Defoe – 1724

Had I not been journeying towards heaven, I could not wish for a more pleasant abiding place than Newcastle.

John Wesley – 1738

An ancient and large town that is exceedingly populous and very rich. It is situated at the end of a wall on the River Tyne, over which it has a fine bridge. The commerce carried on its coals and salmon is amazing, and hath rendered it in great measure of the emporium of the north.

C.T. Middleton – 1778

one

A SHORT HISTORY OF NEWCASTLE UPON TYNE

Newcastle upon Tyne is world famous for the many bridges that span the River Tyne linking the city of Newcastle to Gateshead; the most famous bridge, of course, being the Tyne Bridge.

Work began on the Tyne Bridge in August 1925, and it was completed in 1928. The Tyne Bridge was opened by King George V in that same year. The newest edition to the River Tyne is known as the Millennium Bridge, or the Blinking Eye. On 20 November, in the year 2000, I remember sitting in the garden at my parents' house in Walker – a house that had spectacular views of the river – eagerly awaiting the passing of Asian *Hercules II* that was ferrying the massive 800-tonne structure up the River Tyne from the AMEC Wallsend shipyard where the structure had been assembled. When it eventually passed our house, after its slow and painstaking voyage up the Tyne, I began to comprehend the fact that I was actually experiencing Newcastle's history in the making. It was a day that no one will ever forget.

But it was Emperor Hadrian of the Roman Empire who built the very first bridge that spanned the Tyne – or Tinea, as it was then known – during their occupation of Newcastle around AD 120. The site of the original Roman bridge is roughly where the Swing Bridge now stands. The Roman structure was named Pons Aelii. During the Roman occupation the first fortification that stood in Newcastle was on the site of what is now known as Newcastle Keep. That was named Pons Aelius and it was essentially built to safeguard the bridge Pons Aelii. It was built high on a hill and was the perfect position for such a fortress.

It was AD 122 when the magnificent Hadrian's Wall was built. It was an impressive structure, 10ft wide and 15ft high, that ran nearly seventy-five miles from Bowness on Solway in Cumbria (Maia) to Wallsend (Segedunum). It was built to prevent the military raids from the ancient Scots and Picts, to improve the quality of life and economic stability in the Roman province of Britannia, and in the main to defend the northern frontier. The wall ran straight through Newcastle with Pons Aelius

A small section of Hadrian's Wall on Shields Road, Byker.

being one of its many fortresses; however very little of the wall remains in central Newcastle. There are nevertheless some magnificent remains of the wall and its fortresses further west, stretching across the Pennine Way from Housesteads Roman Fort to Greenheads. A very small section of the wall can be seen in Byker, and the remains of the fort at Segedunum museum where the wall ends is there for everyone to enjoy.

AD 500 saw the Angles arrive in the North East, and Pons Aelius became Monkchester. Although there is very little to support the theory that the Angles occupied Newcastle, there are rumours that there is a Saxon burial ground near to the Roman fortress. After the arrival of William the Conqueror in England in 1066, England was quickly subjected to the Norman rule. In 1080 he sent his son William Curthose north to defend his kingdom against the Scots. It was here where he rebuilt the fortress and a 'New Castle' was erected. It was of motte and bailey construction – essentially a mound of earth on which there is a wooden structure called a keep. It was this castle that gave Newcastle its name. It is also interesting to note that these constructions were called 'grafts' and as they were very hard to construct, the term 'graft', meaning to work hard, came into being.

In 1172 Henry II rebuilt the castle again, this time with stone. It took five years to erect at a cost of £1,000-£1,500. The Black Gate was added to the castle in the reign of Henry III between 1247 and 1250, essentially forming a new Barbican at the north entrance. At this point in time the city walls had yet to be built – when the Scottish

Hadrian's Wall at Housesteads Roman Fort in Northumberland – one of the most magnificent sections of the wall that remains today.

invasions occurred, the townsfolk gathered inside the castle's large, triangular bailey for safety. Throughout the Middle Ages Newcastle was England's most northerly fortress, and after the Battle of Alnwick the Scots' King, William the Lion, was imprisoned there. During the fourteenth century, Newcastle successfully defended its townsfolk on three occasions. The legendary William Wallace, landowner and then a commander in the Scottish Wars of Independence, came through Newcastle with Edward I and, after Wallace's brutal death in London in August 1305, he was hung, drawn and quartered and parts of his body were displayed in Newcastle. His head was then spiked and displayed on London Bridge.

It was also during the Middle Ages that Newcastle's famous city walls were built. In 1265 the town was granted permission to impose a 'wall tax' upon its citizens. This would pay for the construction of a giant, fortified wall that would encompass the town to protect it from further invasions from the marauding Scots. Two miles of city wall were built, consisting of six main gates (with additional smaller ones) and seventeen towers. The wall was 9ft thick and 25ft high. It was an incredible piece of industrialisation. Like the Roman wall, little remains of the town walls, but there are some good sections still left intact which add character, charm and a wonderful historical aspect to what is now a now modern and high-tech municipality.

Established within the city walls were five friaries, the most well known (and the only one that remains standing today) being called Blackfriars. Blackfriars was founded in 1237. Others included Whitefriars (1262), Austinfriars (1290), Greyfriars (1274) and

The city walls stretching west from St Andrew's Church towards Herber Tower.

Herber Tower and the city walls at the west entrance to Chinatown. They head south to Westgate Road.

The Corner Tower on City Road. This section of the wall led to the Sallyport Tower, which stands to the south-east.

A magnificent example of the true height and width of the city walls of Newcastle. This section is located behind the central station on Orchard Street.

the Trinitarians, founded in 1360. There was also one nunnery – St Bartholomew's – founded in 1086 near the city's 'Nun Street'. Of course, the Tudor period began during the 1500s and the dissolution of the monasteries by King Henry VIII led to all of Newcastle's monasteries being dissolved. During the reformation Blackfriars was sub-let to various traders and merchants, and was subsequently used as their headquarters. This is why it survives to this day. By now the wars between the English and the Scots were beginning to diminish and thus the need for the city walls became redundant. They began to decline through lack of maintenance and eventually parts of the walls were demolished and used to make other, new and more needed buildings. During the sixteenth century, Newcastle was also hit by the plague on no more than four occasions, resulting in many deaths. Over 5,000 people in all died as a result of the Black Death.

The city walls were finally breached in 1644 during the Civil War when the Scots once again invaded. Forty thousand Scottish troops besieged Newcastle for almost

The Black Gate, the former entrance to the castle. (Courtesy of Walter Ritson.)

three months until Newcastle's garrison of only 1,500 surrendered. During the siege the Scots bombarded Newcastle and its remaining walls and threatened to destroy the tower of St Nicholas' Cathedral unless the township was surrendered. To counteract this, the Mayor of Newcastle very cunningly filled up the cathedral with Scots prisoners and so saved the building. It was at this point when the King of England at the time – King Charles I – decided to pay homage to the citizens of Newcastle for their bravery and courage by giving Newcastle the motto *Fortiter Defendit Triumphans* (Triumphing by Brave Defence).

In 1715 came the Jacobite Rebellion, followed by a second uprising in 1745 led by Charles Edward Stuart – also known as Bonnie Prince Charlie. Once again Newcastle prepared its defences by re-strengthening the town walls and arresting any Jacobite supporters. Two hundred cannons were deployed, and 20,000 regulars were stationed on Newcastle's Town Moor. This, it seemed, was enough to hold Bonnie Prince Charlie and his army at bay (and as a consequence force them to travel south via England's west coast). It is interesting to add that many believe that the term used for the people of Newcastle is 'Geordie' because King George I was King of England at the time of the rebellion and played a key role in the war. The folk of Newcastle supported the King and were subsequently given the nickname Geordies. In the eighteenth century the term 'German Geordies' was used, as King George was in fact the eldest son of Ernest Augustus, the Duke of Brunswick-Luneburg, who was a German prince.

The year 1787 saw the birth of one John Dobson, and in 1797 Richard Grainger was born. These two men would change the way Newcastle looked forever. They worked together as architects and redeveloped what is now known as Grainger Town in central Newcastle. Present-day Newcastle is adorned with the building work of these two famous sons of the North East. John Dobson designed many of Newcastle's famous buildings, including the Central Station, and Richard Grainger built old Eldon Square. They built Grey Street, Grainger Street, and with the help of John Clayton (born in 1792), they built Clayton Street. The work they carried out in Newcastle was of typical Victorian Gothic style, and wherever one looks in Newcastle you can't help but be reminded of what these people did for the city.

In the year 1854 disaster struck Newcastle upon Tyne and Gateshead in the form of a great fire that ripped through large parts of the river's quaysides. It was said to be the most spectacular and dramatic event in the history of Newcastle and Gateshead. In the early hours of Friday 6 October, at about 3.10 a.m., an explosion rocked a warehouse in Gateshead, sending burning debris shooting off in all directions – which then set fire to everything it touched. They say that the fire would have been serious enough if it had merely been confined to Gateshead, but that was not to be. Newcastle Quayside at that time was the commercial centre of the city and it was almost completely destroyed. It is said that more than fifty people lost their lives and over 200 people were burned out of their homes. Over £500,000 worth of damage was estimated, and in those days that was a lot of money. The fire started at the Worsted manufacturing mill of Wilson & Son and was first spotted by a police officer on duty that night. He gave the alarm immediately, but by the time the fire brigade and police arrived the fire was raging.

St Nicholas' Cathedral at the foot of the Bigg Market. In 1644 the Mayor of Newcastle crammed the tower with Scottish prisoners, effectively saving it from the marauding troops.

Newcastle's motto Fortiter Defendit Triumphans *(Triumphing by Brave Defence), was given to the city by Charles I after the siege of 1644.*

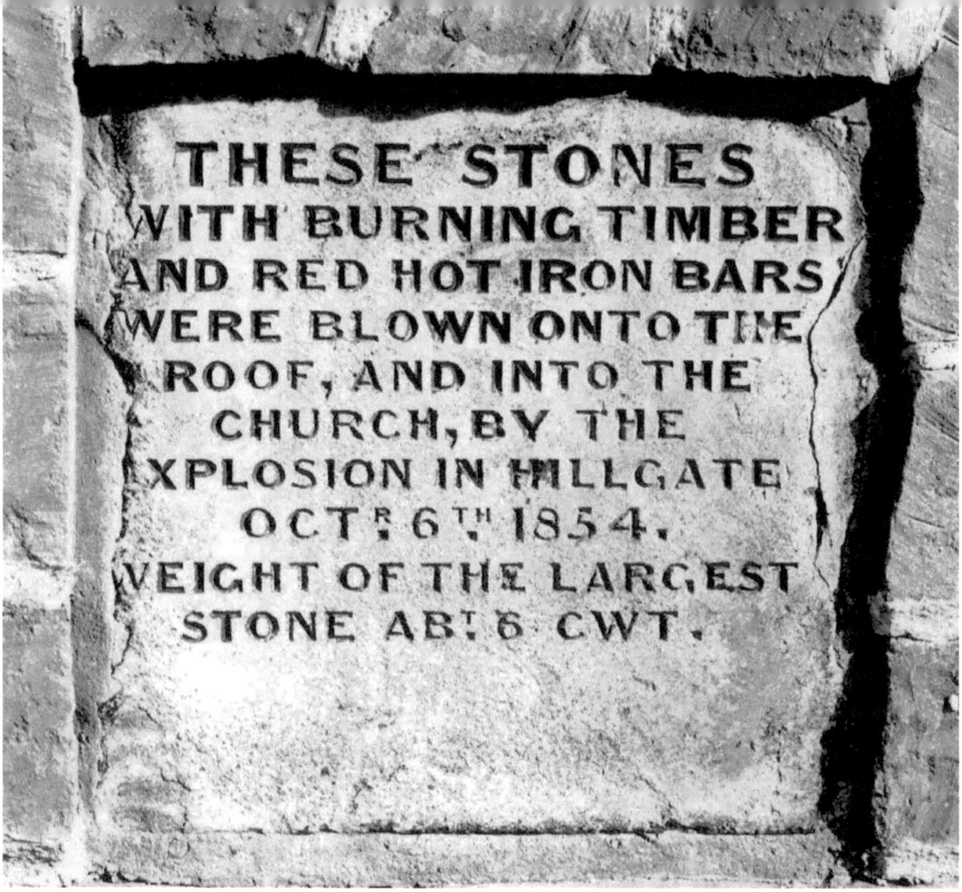

An inscribed stone commemorating the Great Fire of Newcastle and Gateshead in 1854. (Courtesy of Walter Ritson)

By now the fire had drawn large crowds of spectators, and everyone was watching in awe as the fire fighters attempted to bring the blaze under control. Suddenly, an explosion was heard, but it was just a small one that had no effect. Then a second came – it too had no effect, but now the authorities were beginning to worry. Then, their worst fears became a reality when the third explosion occurred: this one was devastating, as on the various floors of the warehouse there were large quantities of sulphur. The heat soon began to melt the sulphur and a purple glow lit up both banks of the Tyne. It sent the debris in all directions, setting fire to all the docked ships on Newcastle Quayside and parts of Gateshead, resulting in the worst disaster that Newcastle and Gateshead has ever seen. In Newcastle the force of the explosion blew out all the windows of the shops in the Sandhill area of the Quayside as well as other places too. Dean Street, Mosley Street, Grey Street, Pilgrim Street, Market Street and even Clayton Street were affected by the blast.

The explosion was said to be so powerful that nearby boats literally shook, the old stone bridge trembled and the boom was heard many, many miles away. The flames could allegedly be seen fifty miles south of the blaze near Northallerton, while the explosion was heard in Hexham. Those in Sunderland believed the blast was on their own doorstep, and at a paper factory in Jarrow the gas lamps were blown

The severely damaged quayside after the Great Fire of 1854. (Courtesy of Newcastle Libraries and Information Service)

out by the blast. This just gives an indication of how disastrous the explosion and resulting fires were.

Although many died in the fire there are numerous stories of lucky escapes and survival. Some people were extremely lucky to have survived such a fire, but they did. Many accounts came in, such as one chap who was blown under a bridge with great force and was completely unhurt. Another fellow jumped from a burning building as it collapsed under him and lived to tell the tale. One man had heard all the commotion and got out of his bed to see what was happening. At that very second, the flying debris hit a gable wall of his house, which collapsed upon his bed – the bed he was sleeping in moments earlier. These and many more miracles happened on that fateful night.

One of the dead, however, was the second son of Newcastle architect John Dobson, Alexander R. Dobson, aged only twenty-five. The search for bodies after the fire went on for several days, and those recovered were only identified from their personal belongings. In Dobson's case, it was his bunch of keys that revealed his identity. To this day, no one knows for sure how the fire or the following explosions started, although there were a few theories at the time. Detailed analysis of the warehouses and the contents contained therein yielded no results, and there was no indication of arson. I guess it will remain in the history of Gateshead and Newcastle as not only the worst fire of it kind, but one of the most mysterious too.

In 1778, Newcastle upon Tyne was described by C.T. Middleton as, 'an ancient and large town that is exceedingly populous and very rich. It is situated at the end of a wall on the River Tyne, over which it has a fine bridge. The commerce carried on its coals and salmon is amazing, and hath rendered it in great measure of the emporium of the north'.

It was a beautiful town, but this was to change in some measure over the next 100 years. Newcastle upon Tyne in the late 1800s was by then the chief port of the great Northern Coalfield and was well known and acknowledged worldwide. However, it was only the coal-mining industry that outsiders recognised, and an imprecise notion of Newcastle upon Tyne was that of an immense pit heap in which its trade and commerce consisted of nothing more than mining and shipping coal. In this respect, Newcastle was – by way of an analogy – like the famous poet Campbell, who would often complain that nobody wanted to know him or speak with him except when they wanted to discuss his book *Pleasures of Hope*. Everything else he had ever done was hitherto overlooked and ignored, and for this reason Campbell was deeply saddened. If Newcastle had never begun its mining industry and had never shipped any coal abroad, Newcastle as a city would have been relatively unknown and off the radar, so to speak.

Newcastle upon Tyne, however, did have other industries that would also have given it a respectable claim to nobility. The banks of the River Tyne were adorned with

The Quayside viewed from Gateshead after the Great Fire of 1854. The scale of the damage is clearly evident. (Courtesy of Newcastle Libraries and Information Service)

industries such as iron, engineering and chemical works, and of course shipbuilding (which it is still famous for to this day). Nevertheless, known for its grim and dangerous hard work, Newcastle was contemptuously ignored by those who visited other picturesque cities and towns. Thus Newcastle, in effect, became a leper amongst towns.

Bringing it up to date, Newcastle upon Tyne in the new millennium is one of the most wonderful cities on the planet. But don't take my word for it! With many fantastic attractions, fine night-life, good shopping, events, festival, arts and culture, is it any wonder that Newcastle upon Tyne was a top contender for the title of European City of Culture?

I will conclude this section at this particular juncture as I have endeavoured to keep this segment relatively short. However, a mixture of the respective sections that follow in this volume will of course have their own historical aspects detailed. Should the reader wish to learn more regarding the history of Newcastle upon Tyne, I would recommend they consult the bibliography at the back of this book.

two

THE GHOSTS OF AN ANCIENT CITY

Theatre Ghosts

Where better to start a ghost tour of haunted Newcastle than at a theatre? There are a number of theatres in the city, but the two most well known are said to house denizens of the other world. Of course, it has become almost a cliché that theatres are haunted and every theatre in the land lays claim to having its resident ghost. It's as though these fantastic old entertainment auditoriums are not complete unless they have a grey man wandering the isles, or a phantom artiste who still performs upon their ethereal stages. The theatre ghost has now become part of the fixtures and fittings, and behind every ghost there is nearly always an account of a tragedy.

The first establishment I wish to tell the reader about is the Tyne Theatre on Westgate Road, and believe me when I say there are no more tragic circumstances than in this case. I first remember hearing about the ghost on a school trip to the theatre many, many years ago. We were told that an employee – a man named Robert – was standing by the stage one day. Suddenly, from out of nowhere came a cannonball that hit him on the top of the head, caving in his skull and ultimately killing him. The cannonball was kept very high above the stage and was used as a prop to create a thunder effect during certain performances. With its weight, it had fallen through the old wooden receptacle that it was kept in – about 15ft above the stage – and plummeted to earth with incredible speed. Robert, or Bob, as he was known, was in the wrong place at the wrong time. Since that awful event there has been a terrible sense of sadness … and a presence felt at the theatre.

His restless ghost is said to wander the stage area where he died, as well as in other parts of the theatre where he worked. He is also reputed to have had a favourite seat within the theatre stalls and has been spotted sitting in it from time to time.

The Theatre Royal on Grey Street, opened on 20 February 1837, is fine example of John and Benjamin Green's architecture; it fits in well with Grainger Town. The theatre is said to be haunted by the ghost of a suicidal woman known as the Grey Lady.

Theatre Royal and Grey's Monument.

Grainger Town. Newcastle is adorned with architecture such as this – all one has to do to see it is simply to look up.

The ghost of a woman, known as the Grey Lady, is also said to haunt the theatre, although details of her demise (and why she haunts here) are rather vague. Some say she was jilted by her lover and threw herself to her death from the gallery; others say she fell by accident. No one knows for sure.

I take you now to the most famous and by far the most spectacular theatre in Tyneside – the Theatre Royal on Grey Street. The theatre is a Grade I listed building that was constructed in the early 1830s. It was officially opened on 20 February 1837 (although Newcastle's first Theatre Royal was actually opened on 21 January 1788). This original Theatre Royal was housed on Mosley Street. The present Theatre Royal was designed by local architects to fit in with Richard Grainger's wonderful 'Grainger Town'. John and Benjamin Green were a father-and-son team, and designed many of Newcastle's famous buildings and landmarks (such as the Literary and Philosophical Society that stands at the foot of Westgate Road, and Grey's Monument at the top of Grey Street). The theatre on Grey Street is another of their masterpieces.

The tale of the ghost of the Theatre Royal, however, is very a hackneyed account; indeed it bares a striking resemblance to the account from the Tyne Theatre, which begs the question 'is the story a genuine one and, if so, to which theatre does it really belong?' It appears that the Theatre Royal also lays claim to a Grey Lady and she, like the ghost of the Tyne Theatre, threw herself from the upper gallery and killed herself. Again, details are scant – and yet the legend seems to live on.

The Assembly Rooms on Fenkle Street, built in 1776 and said to be haunted by the ghost of a woman who threw herself to her death from a balcony.

The Assembly Rooms

The site now occupied by the present-day Assembly Rooms was first used as Newcastle's original Assembly House From 1716-1736. At the same time it was also used as a school for girls. Presently, the Assembly Rooms in Newcastle are located on the same site on Fenkle Street, which is just off Westgate Road. It dates back to 1776, although the actual foundation-stone for the new building was laid in 1774 after decisions were made to remodel and rebuild. It is now one of the finest examples of Georgian Newcastle and was designed by the eminent Newcastle architect William Newton.

This one-time casino has played host to many notable visitors during the course of its wonderful past, including George V and Queen Mary in 1928, to coincide with the opening of the Tyne Bridge. Edward III visited the rooms during his time in Newcastle in 1906, and a ball was held there for the Duke of Wellington back in 1827. Charles Dickens also performed his plays here, and the rooms have also played host to world-famous composers such as Johann Strauss and Franz Liszt.

The story that is said to account for the spectre there is an interesting one, and begins in the late 1700s where, it was said, a party was being held in the upper sections of the Assembly Rooms. It is believed that during these festivities the wife of one of the party-goers was made to dance in the nude for his other drunken friends. This she did – very reluctantly – but felt great shame afterwards. It is then said she crept away

Friars Green at Blackfriars Monastery. Here the ghost of a monk has been seen wandering aimlessly around at night. (Courtesy of Darren Olley)

from the party and threw herself from one of the upper balconies to her death. Is the ghost of the Assembly Rooms and this distressed and embarrassed lady one and the same? Members of staff and visitors alike have reported seeing the ghost, and the area where she is said to have landed after her fall is where sudden cold spots and a 'sense of a presence' is often felt.

Blackfriars Monastery

Blackfriars Monastery is tucked away neatly behind the city's Chinatown, and is now a thriving tourist centre and beauty spot. On many afternoons I have meandered down to the ruins for a few relaxing hours in the sunshine, and to generally take in the ambience of the locale. It is a wonderful place to spend time and is a veritable oasis in the midst of a hectic conurbation.

Blackfriars Monastery is a thirteenth-century Dominican friary and was founded by a very wealthy merchant called Sir Peter Scott. In those days Dominican friars were not allowed to own property, and such places of inhabitation were often held in trust for them. Blackfriars was no exception. The friary covered almost seven acres of land, including a number of gardens, in which the friars could spend time working. During the nineteenth and twentieth centuries the building was badly neglected and fell into serious disrepair. Now, only the cloisters remain of the original friary and the stone

An engraved stone that is located over the archway entrance reads: 'By hammer and hand all arts do stand'.

outline of the church that once belonged there can be observed in the grassy area of the complex known as Friars Green.

In the early 1950s the Newcastle Corporation acquired the site and in the 1970s and 1980s it was subsequently brought back to life. Nowadays the buildings are used as craft workshops, tea and coffee shops and general stores along with a wonderful exhibition on the upper floor of the front of the complex that details the history of the friary. On a nice sunny day at the old friary you can relax in the wonderful surroundings that are steeped with history. However, when night-time falls the atmosphere begins to take a sinister turn, and after the last of the in-house shops are closed up and locked for the night, and the visitors have long since gone, it is said the ghost monk of Blackfriars makes his appearance.

Legend has it that a monk from Blackfriars and a nun from the nearby Covent of St Bartholomew (in what is now Nun Street) committed the ultimate sin, and many indiscretions took place between the two. Eventually, this resulted in the unwanted pregnancy of the nun. The nun was allegedly bricked up alive in the convent and subsequently starved to death, while the fate of the culpable monk is said to be unknown. However, it is his ghost that is thought to be the wandering phantom that walks the grounds of the former friary – perhaps in torment at the death of his lover and her child.

An artist's impression depicting a ghost monk that is said to walk the ruins. (Illustration by Julie Olley)

His ghost has been seen countless times at night over the years and, on occasions, during the day. Staff at the tearooms and shops have reported seeing a hunched, browbeaten figure moving within the building and disappearing into thin air in the middle of Friars Green. Others claim to have seen only half of the monk – from the waist up – as he walks on the original ground level in and across Friars Green. Objects have been moved around and a dark figure has been seen in the old friary's banqueting hall (which is now a large tea room).

On one occasion not so long ago, during one of my many visits there, I made it my business to speak to a number of shop proprietors in my search for recent paranormal events. The owner of one wonderfully cram-packed knick-knack store informed me that he had experienced something that he would have described as 'paranormal' in his little shop.

He went on to tell me that he thought the idea of sharing his business with a resident ghost was absolutely enchanting and welcomed the presence in his store. He would often find the light in his shop turned on in the mornings after leaving it off the night before. Key-rings and such-like that hang up on stands would be heard to 'rattle' as if someone had brushed past them, but there was never anybody there – no one he could see, anyway. On one occasion he heard footsteps on the shop floor and, thinking it was a customer, he looked up to serve them only to find the shop

The front porch and tower of St Andrew's Church. There are two mysteries associated with St Andrew's: the witches' bones and the ghost girl.

completely empty. After I drank my cup of tea that was so kindly prepared for me, I made my way out of Blackfriars. It is indeed a wonderful place to go and visit and I recommend you all go there yourself sometime even if for just an hour or so – you never know, you might even see the sad ghost of the monk.

7 Old Eldon Square

Old Eldon Square was designed, built and completed by Richard Grainger in or around 1830 and it is one of Newcastle's most attractive areas in regards to city architecture. It is near Grey's Monument and opposite the bus station on Blackett Street. For years the square (or the Hippy Green, as it became known) was used on Saturday afternoons by the city's Goth population who would gather to simply chill out and spend time in the sunshine. Situated in the centre of the square is Charles Hartwell's magnificent mounted statue of George and the Dragon, which was erected in 1923.

It is also at this location that a sad haunting is said to have once taken place. A ghost of a young girl is said to have been heard – but not seen – on the top floor of the premises of 7 Old Eldon Square. The ghost is alleged to have been heard laughing and talking softly to herself while playing in the attic room of the building. A shop assistant, while working in the property, witnessed the ghostly occurrences. The assistant's duties included re-stocking the shop from the storerooms on the top floor and it was when this duty was being carried out the ghostly encounters occurred. No one knows whom the girl was or why she is said to have haunted the building.

St Andrew's Churchyard

There are two mysteries surrounding the church of St Andrew, one being the ghost of the vanishing girl and the other that of the mystery bones believed to be the remains of a witch. The church, which is situated on the corner of Newgate Street, is said to be the oldest church in Newcastle and dates back to the twelfth century. It is believed that St Andrew's Church stands on the site of a far older building, possibly another church or a Roman building. The latest addition to this wonderful old church was in 1726, when the front porch was added.

The church even played its part in the Civil War when a cannon was mounted on the original church tower in an effort to help defend the city. The Newcastle city walls once stood next to the church, and some remains of it can still be seen today. This made the tower an ideal location for the huge gun. However, in 1644, during the Scottish invasion, much of the church was damaged, to the point where it became redundant and not used for over a year. When work began to restore St Andrew's it was subsequently modified and altered.

A friend of mine (ironically called Andrew) told me that his father was the caretaker here at St Andrew's and spent many a lonely hour in the building and church, often at night, tending to his duties. On many occasions he would feel he was not on his own

The graves in St Andrew's churchyard where the ghost girl has been seen running through the graves.

and often had the impression that he was being watched, although no ghost sightings were ever reported inside the church. Outside in the grounds, however, it is a different story. The ghost that is said to be seen here is that of a young girl. The story goes that an adolescent trainee priest fell in love with the daughter of a wealthy landowner and was to meet up with her one night near the church. When he arrived he spotted her meandering in a daze around the churchyard and wondered why she looked this way. The trainee priest then allegedly darted into the churchyard to catch up with her, but she ran away from him and disappeared in front of his eyes. Puzzled by this event he went home and retired for the night, mulling over in his head what he had seen.

It was not until the following day that he learned that his beloved girlfriend had been seriously ill and had actually died the night before – and at the exact time he saw her in the graveyard. How strange it was that he should see her ghost before her actual death. Known as ghosts of the living, or crisis apparitions, this haunting – to my knowledge – is the only one of its kind in Newcastle. Not long after the girl's sad death, reports began to come in of a phantom girl, wearing a long, flowing gown, running through the graveyard, only to disappear into the ether – very similar to what had been witnessed the night before her death. Not only was she a ghost before her death, it seems she was a ghost afterwards too.

The second mystery in regards to the church came about quite recently when some bone fragments were found in the graveyard. Builders discovered part of a skull, a rib, and some teeth – believed to be the remains of hanged witches – during their work there. Records show that around sixteen so-called witches were buried in a pit at St Andrew's churchyard after being hanged on Newcastle's Town Moor on 21 August 1650. It is believed the bones that were found may well belong to some of them.

An interesting postscript follows the discovery of the mystery bones at St Andrew's. It is said that one of the workers came across a bone fragment, picked it up and showed it to his colleagues. The next day his arm was covered in scabs and sores, and when he went to the doctors to get some treatment, they could not diagnose his condition; nor could they work out how or why they had appeared. Since then, the witches' bones have been labelled 'cursed' and now people refuse to touch them. Whether or not they are really cursed witches' bones I guess we will never know, but it is an interesting story nonetheless.

Roman Around the Keep

Now for a short and very odd account: the ghost sighting of a Roman soldier seen outside Newcastle Keep one night. It occurred prior to a research team carrying out an overnight investigation there a few years ago. I was part of an investigative team (now disbanded) that was running the investigation and our special guest for the evening just happened to be the lady who actually saw the ghost. It also must be stressed that she is a renowned television medium.

The Keep of the New Castle, from which the city takes its name. It was built on the site of a Roman settlement and very haunted indeed.

After she and her husband arrived she got out of her car and said hello to everyone. She then began to take a walk around the castle, and her senses were obviously working overtime. After she walked around the base of the castle she told us that she had seen a Roman soldier standing at the foot of the castle walls looking, in her words, 'lost'. Other sightings of Roman soldiers have been reported in this area, and I needn't remind the reader (although I am about to) that this area was once a Roman settlement called Pons Aelius. Coincidence? I think not, although why the soldier would look lost eludes me. Nonetheless, I believe she really did see the ghost of a Roman. It has happened here before, and I am sure it will happen again – the only question is when. You just never know, it could be you who sees it next time.

The Phantom Cavalier of Sallyport Tower

Standing majestically overlooking the Pandon district of Newcastle is the Sallyport Tower. Situated on Tower Street, which is at the west end of City Road, the Sallyport Tower was one of the seventeen towers that surrounded Newcastle as part of the defence system that was known as the city walls. This particular tower is the only one that is still more-or-less intact, though a lot of the original tower cannot be seen due to it being added to and altered over the years. Buildings do unfortunately corrode over the years, and these repairs were necessary in order to preserve to the original

The Sallyport Tower on Tower Street is said to be haunted by a Civil War soldier who stares out from one of the windows.

An artist's impression of a ghost soldier as he looks out of a window, similar to the ghost of Sallyport Tower. (Illustration by Julie Olley)

tower; it is there – we just can't see it. One thing that has remained at the Sallyport Tower for many, many years is the ghost of the Sallyport Cavalier.

This fearless warrior was said to have departed from this life after a major siege by the Scots in 1644. His shade – so they say – is seen quite often staring out from inside one of the tower windows, perhaps still looking out from his post and carrying out his duty of defending the city he so loved. One witness said that she had watched in awe as he glided in an upwards direction from below the window and up through the ceiling. This was where a spiral staircase was said to have been. What puzzles me is the fact that if the soldier was making his way upstairs on the spirals, wouldn't he have been seen to walk up the stairs (all be they invisible) like one would in real life? Wouldn't he have had his knees bending and his back slowly turning upon the witness as he ascended, and not just merely floating in an upward direction?

To me this account doesn't hold any validity, but that's not to say it did not occur. I am simply expressing my opinion. The notion of the phantom looking out of the window is far more plausible, but one needs to remember that the floor he once would have stood upon to peer out of the windows is now long gone, and today the windows in the tower are very high up indeed. The ghost of the Sallyport Tower has not been seen for quite some time now, and one wonders if he is at rest knowing that he has fulfilled his duties as a sentry. Or perhaps he is lying dormant, waiting for the next siege of Newcastle so he can return once again and defend our noble city.

The many wonderful arches of the Holy Jesus Hospital. The building, previously known as the Joicey Museum, was once subjected to all sorts of strange and unexplained phenomena. However, nowadays all seems to be quiet.

The Holy Jesus Hospital

The Holy Jesus Hospital is located just off the Swan House roundabout to the east on City Road in central Newcastle, and is a short distance from the Sallyport Tower. Between 1971 and 1994, the building was also known as the Joicey Museum. The Holy Jesus Hospital dates back to 1681 and it is said to be one of only two seventeenth-century buildings to survive in Newcastle today. At the north-east corner, standing tall, there is a much earlier construction in the form of a fourteenth-century tower that was said to be part of the Augustinian Priory that once stood there on that spot.

The building is currently occupied by the National Trust's Inner City Project, which is essentially a charity that introduces people from the inner-city areas to the natural beauty of the countryside. The Inner City Project has been based at the Holy Jesus Hospital for many years now, and began in 1987.

A local newspaper once ran a feature about the ghosts of the Holy Jesus Hospital and it went into some detail as to what had been reported there. Doors would open and close on their own, and often be found unlocked when staff had previously locked them. On other occasions the phenomena would be reversed, as unlocked doors would then be found closed and locked. Apparitions have been reported there too, one being a hooded figure in dark or black robes that has been seen both inside and outside the building. There is also the ghost of a woman with a long dress who has been seen in one of the rooms which is now probably used as an office.

A rear view of the Holy Jesus Hospital with the fourteenth-century Augustinian Tower.

I visited the Holy Jesus Hospital during my research and spoke to the property manager, Gerrard New, and another member of staff, Raymond Cross, in order to try to gain more information regarding the ghosts that are said to reside here. I was subsequently informed that although they were open to the idea of ghosts, they had experienced absolutely nothing during their time there. Neither had they even heard of the building being haunted or about its spooky reputation. This pointed towards a number of possibilities: either no paranormal experiences had been observed for a long while simply because its residing ghosts had chosen not to show themselves (for whatever reason), or, as in some cases, the alleged activity that was once witnessed there ceased after a while. It is very common for ghosts to be seen and heard only once or twice in the space of 100 years or so. A third possibility could be Holy Jesus Hospital is not actually haunted at all, which in all honesty could be the reality of it … I guess we will never know unless a new sighting is documented, until which I wait with baited breath.

All Saints' Church

All Saints' Church is located at the foot of Pilgrim Street to the east of the Tyne Bridge, and stands proudly at the top of a steep embankment which commands spectacular views over the Quayside and the Pandon area of the city. This elegant construction, with a tower soaring just over 200ft, dates back to 1796 and was built upon the site of the original Church of All Saints. One of the city's most famous spectres is well known in the Pandon area and goes by the name of Jack the Beadle. The story of Jack the Beadle was told to the youngsters in the late nineteenth century in an effort to deter misbehaviour. They were informed that if they were seen to be up to mischief, Jack's spirit would turn up and take them away – and they wouldn't be seen again.

The story originated in 1858 when the Beadle of All Saints' Church had been caught stealing lead from recently buried coffins and selling it on for his own personal gain. This was unacceptable behaviour for anyone, never mind the parish constable who was responsible for the upkeep and general maintenance of the church and grounds! This was a position of trust that was grossly misused and so he was given a punishment of nearly two years hard labour – and in those days this really did mean hard labour. After his death rumours began to circulate that his restless ghost was seen at night in the churchyard of All Saints, prowling around in the darkness with his lit lantern. He is said to be either looking for more lead to steal and sell, or perhaps lurking in wait for the mischievous children, ready to pounce on them and whisk them away.

All Saints' Church at the bottom of Pilgrim Street. (Courtesy of Darren Olley)

An artists' impression of Jack the Beadle as he prowls the churchyard. (Illustration by Julie Olley)

St Nicholas' Cathedral

Located at the top of the Side, and next to Amen Corner, St Nicholas' Cathedral stands proudly dominating the Newcastle skyline. Known as 'the Mother Church of the Diocese of Newcastle', St Nicholas' Cathedral dates back to the twelfth century, although it has only been recognised as a cathedral since the nineteenth century. Prior to that, it was known as St Nicholas' Church. In 1644 the building could have been completely demolished had it not been for the quick thinking of the Mayor of Newcastle; as I mentioned in the introduction, he was ordered to surrender the city during the siege, or the cathedral would be fired upon. Instead, he rounded up all the Scottish prisoners and forced them into the tower, thus saving it from the Scottish guns. Inside the cathedral there are many wonderful memorials and artefacts, including a wonderful stone effigy of an unknown knight from the thirteenth century that lies in an alcove in the west wall.

Interestingly enough, it is said a ghost of a knight complete with armour has been seen inside the cathedral near to where the 'unknown knight's effigy' lies. One American holidaymaker, who was staying in the city for a while back in the 1980s, took numerous photographs of the cathedral inside and out. Upon her return home to the USA, she found to her surprise a faint figure of what looked like a knight

An image of Newcastle Keep with St Nicholas' Cathedral in the background. (Courtesy of Walter Ritson)

The effigy of the unknown knight dating from the thirteenth century that rests in St Nicholas' Cathedral.

Knights' graves in Amen Corner. (Courtesy of Walter Ritson)

standing among some chairs on the inside of the cathedral. Tests proved the picture was genuine, but my efforts to try and track the tourist down to see the picture (and perhaps re-produce it here) came to nothing.

Auditory phenomena have also been heard inside the cathedral too, with the sounds of metal 'clinking' and 'clanking' reverberating around the echoic interior. No explanations have ever been suggested for the metallic-sounding anomalies, but some suggest it is the ghost of the knight pacing the stone floors in an attempt to be noticed. Perhaps it is.

El-Torero Restaurant and Milburn House

The El-Torero Spanish restaurant is located on Newcastle upon Tyne's 'Side', which runs down to the Quayside behind the Black Gate. Not much is known about the actual history of the restaurant other than that it was another restaurant prior to that, and – when the building was constructed in 1905 – this particular spot was both a post office and a bank. We also know that the actual building it is housed in runs up the 'Side', and is called Milburn House. The head of the Side was once railway viaducts, which led to the corner of Milburn House. The old viaduct ran straight through where the building is now situated to Amen Corner, which is next to Newcastle's great cathedral.

Milburn House.

The Vampire Rabbit of Milburn House.

Milburn House was built with funding from the Milburn family and, because of their connection with shipping, the floors are labelled, deck-style, with 'A' at the top and 'G' on the ground floor. On 26 September 1748, Admiral Lord Collingwood was born in a house located somewhere on this particular site; where, exactly, no one is sure. Could he been have born in a house that is now the El-Torero restaurant? Could his ghost still wander aimlessly in the place he once called home?

Since the El-Torero restaurant began its business at these premises in 2001, the owners and staff have become convinced that it is haunted. On a number of occasions an invisible presence has been sensed by the staff, leaving them quite on edge to say the least! A lady who once worked here heard her name being called out, though she was the only one on the premises. Thinking she wasn't alone after all, she replied to the voice, only to have no one answer back. She stopped working and looked around to see who it was, but the room was empty. All the doors were locked. This phenomenon is often documented during a haunting and is actually more common than people think. Then there are the sightings of a ghost-lady who has been seen in one of the mirrors in the restaurant. The restaurant is a fabulous little place to eat out and is one of Newcastle's hidden gems. Out of general interest, this particular restaurant plays a large part in Newcastle's famous ghost-walks.

During my research into the ghosts of El-Torero I was subsequently informed of a resident spectre that has been seen wandering aimlessly inside the corridors of this magnificent old edifice. One witness claims to have seen the hazy apparition of an old man with a stick making his way towards one of the closed doors in the corridor – he vanished into thin air before he reached the door. Research turned up no records of previous sightings of this ghost, so one presumes it never made the newspapers. Hearsay and rumour is all we have to go on with this alleged ghost and nothing as yet has been validated – unlike the first-hand accounts of the ghosts of El-Torero.

Around the corner and perched high a doorway to a solicitor's office stands the Vampire Rabbit of Newcastle. No one really knows why it is there and as far as I know there are no folklore or ghost tales connected to it. It has pointed ears standing to attention, blood-red claws that grip the top of the doorway, bloodstained fangs gaping from its mouth and piercing red eyes. The rabbit stares down upon you with a look that sends chills down the spine.

The Quayside Silky of Trinity Chare

One of Newcastle's most terrifying spectres is known as 'the Quayside silky'. A silky is the customary name for a female apparition that can be seen, but more often heard due to the rustling of her silk dress or clothes. This apparition hasn't been seen for many, many years now and the area which she haunts, although slightly changed in recent years, is still more-or-less intact. The old word 'chare' means alleyway, or 'side street', and the Quayside has many of them, the most well known being Broad Chare and Trinity Chare.

An old view of the Sandgate area of the Quayside in 1881. (Courtesy of Newcastle Libraries and Information Service)

Broad Chare.

Broad Chare is located next to the law courts near the Millennium Bridge and runs up to the road that joins the Tyne Bridge near the All Saints' Church. Trinity Chare, where the silky is said to haunt, is a little further down the Quayside. While I was looking at an old map of the city from 1736 with Paul McDonald (curator of Newcastle Keep), I discovered that Trinity Chare was actually called Rencastle Chare. This particular silky is said to be a mischievous spectre that frightens the living daylights out of anyone that chances to encounter her. No one knows why she haunts this area, but there were stories of a suicide linked to nearby Trinity House, although nothing is substantiated. Used as the headquarters for the Maritime Organisation, Trinity House is an establishment that is committed to the wellbeing of sailors and to the safe course-plotting of those in the naval trades; it has been doing so since it was built in 1505.

The story dates back to the early 1800s when it was said that an old local woman called Martha Wilson was found hanged in a dwelling close by. The dwelling was known as an almshouse and it was an abode that was bestowed by Trinity House to the local poor folk in the elderly community at that time. Because it was believed she had committed suicide her body was not interred in consecrated grounds but buried at a crossroads in the vicinity; no one knows where exactly. A lot of alleged hauntings are said to be induced by this very aspect so perhaps this haunting is no different.

An image of where Broad Chare meets the Quayside in the 1980s. (Courtesy of Walter Ritson)

Trinity Chare, where the faceless silky is said to scare you witless should you ever run into her. However, she hasn't been seen for many years now.

However, the thought occurs that Martha may have actually been murdered and subsequently haunts the area seeking justice for her brutal demise.

One tale of the silky caught my attention while reading a short but fascinating book called *Dark Tales of Old Newcastle*. In it, the author tells us that one dark night a keelman was on his way home after a night in the local taverns when he became aware that a woman was following him on the other side of the road. She seemed to be moving along at the same pace as he was until she reached Trinity Chare. She then disappeared up the alleyway and into the darkness. The keelman had been aware of the tales of phantoms generally known as the silky and was sceptical about them. Nevertheless, he was compelled to follow her into Trinity Chare. He thought there was something distinctly odd about this woman and I guess his curiosity got the better of him. As he approached the mysterious woman from behind, she stopped and turned towards him. This halted the now terrified keelman in his tracks and a stand-off then ensued. The keelman took a short step towards the woman, and as he got closer he realised that there was no head beneath the woman's veil.

Comprehending what he saw before him, the keelman turned and ran out of Trinity Chare, accompanied by the harrowing shriek of her evil laughter.

The Trinity House Almshouse where Martha Wilson is said to have lived.

Bessie Surtees House and Dog Leap Stairs

A wonderful story of unrequited love leads us into our next ghost story and begins in the early 1770s. John Scott, the first Earl of Eldon and Lord Chancellor of Great Britain, fell deeply in love with a woman called Bessie Surtees who was the eldest daughter of Aubone Surtees, a Newcastle banker. The Surtees family objected to the couple's relationship and Bessie was forbidden to see her lover. This, however, did not stop the couple from eloping as John Scott hatched an astute plan. Bessie had been confined to a room by her family (in what is now Bessie Surtees house, which was named after her) in an effort to prevent her liaisons with John Scott. It was from this room that Bessie made her escape after John Scott waited outside on horseback. With the help of a friend and a ladder, Bessie climbed out of the window and on to the back of John Scott's steed.

During the escape Bessie Surtees family became aware of what was happening and an effort was made to bring this situation under control. John Scott and Bessie Surtees galloped away on horseback closely followed by two or three of Bessie's family on their horses. John and Bessie galloped around the corner and along a road known as The Side until they reached a long and steep flight of stairs now known as Dog Leap

The window from which Bessie Surtees made her daring escape in 1772.

Dog Leap Stairs, said to be haunted by the sound of Galloping horses.

Stairs. Without hesitation John geared the horse and attempted to scale the stairs on horseback. Anyone that has ever seen Dog Leap Stairs will know that to attempt to ride a horse to the top successfully is nigh-on impossible, yet somehow John and Bessie made it.

Those in pursuit of John and Bessie, however, did not. After getting half way up the stairs the horses could take no more and subsequently fell backwards down on to the steep and narrow stone stairwell. This saw the end of the pursuit (and resulted in the deaths of some of the horses and their riders). John and Bessie continued their elopement over the Scottish border to Blackshields where they married and lived peacefully for the rest of their lives.

On many occasions the ghostly sounds of phantom horses and their galloping hooves have been heard ascending the stone stairs. This auditory phenomenon seems to peak mid-way up the long flight of stairs, so one can surmise that this could well be the spot the horses and their riders reached before plummeting back down again. Soaring brick walls stand high on either side of the steep stairwell, thus resulting in the intensification of normal sounds – and the ghostly ones. It is said that the noises of these phantom horses cannot be mistaken by those who have heard them, and from what I have been told they sound incredibly real. In fact, I was told they are 'so real' I set out one day to attempt to record them.

Dog Leap Stairs.

An old alleyway near The Side in 1978. (Courtesy of Walter Ritson)

I made a number of tape recordings on the stairs while simultaneously listening out for any acoustics that may well be interpreted as galloping horses. I thought maybe the way the stairs are built, combined with the tall walls on either side of them, may somehow produce sound that could somehow be described as hooves on concrete. I heard nothing. I sat there all day and recorded absolutely nothing. But that is ghost hunting!

The Haunted Pizza Shop – Bigg Market

Opposite the KFC at the top left-hand corner of the Bigg Market stands (at the time of writing) a Pizza Hut. This particular building made news in the late 1990s and in early 2000 when the ghost of a young Victorian boy was repeatedly seen in the basement. The ghost was seen standing silently in the lower section of the shop, then, after a few seconds, he vanished into thin air.

I remember popping in one day for a pizza at the time of the alleged hauntings – a 'seafood special' if I remember rightly – and enquiring about the ghost sightings. I chatted with an employee who had worked there for a while and was subsequently informed that although he hadn't seen the spectre he knew someone that did – a former work colleague. Unfortunately, I was told, this individual left his student job after he saw the apparition. I was unsuccessful in ascertaining the name of this one-time employee and it was my only chance, perhaps, to speak to an actual eye-witness. The employee I spoke too did say, however, that he felt 'uneasy' when down in the basement. He then pointed me over in the direction of the store manager who went on to tell me that he 'always felt as though I'm being watched when I go down into the basement … perhaps it's a result of already knowing the room is supposed to be haunted'. I for one agreed with him.

This information was gleaned nearly ten years ago, and I was fortunate enough to have found the interviews that I had carried out at the time in my archives at home. I now thought it was time to update the story, so I paid another visit to the premises in 2008. Almost ten years on I find that although the reputation of the ghost boy in the basement still lingers on, the ghost itself does not. I was informed that he has not been seen at all as far as the counter assistant could tell me, leaving the other current employees rather sceptical about the whole episode. Whether he does still appear or not, the fact of the matter is that a Victorian boy was seen back in the late 1990s and early 2000, begging the questions that will most likely never be answered – who was he, and why did he haunt the basement?

'Tom' of The Bigg Market

In early 2008 I was contacted by a young lady called Gemma Gorner who claimed she was living in a haunted apartment in the centre of Newcastle. She went on to inform me that she was given my contact details by Paul McDonald (the curator of

The Pizza Hut in the Bigg Market was once haunted by the ghost of a Victorian boy, seen in the cellars (now Pasta Hut).

Newcastle Keep) after visiting there one day. She had noticed some of my previous books that were on sale at the Keep and mentioned to Paul that she too had 'a ghost'. Paul then very kindly offered my services and for this I am indebted to him. Gemma was more than willing to tell me about the alleged ghost in her house. Although there had indeed been a few 'odd incidences' reported by Gemma and her housemates, I felt a visit was not yet warranted. The usual array of phenomena had been witnessed – such as strange noises, objects seemingly being moved around and footsteps being heard inside the property when no one else was there. In all honesty, I thought that as she lived with four of her student friends maybe a lot of the reported phenomena were caused by themselves (though they might not have realised that they were the cause).

On 30 May 2008, I was contacted once more with information that the ghost was up to its old tricks, only this time it had become worse. I was informed that noises were frequently being heard while Gemma was 'in the flat on her own'. When I asked her to elaborate upon what exactly she had heard I must admit it sounded strikingly similar to a poltergeist case that I had investigated in the summer of 2006. I was informed that one afternoon while Gemma was home alone a loud noise was heard. I was told, 'It sounded like a large spoon being thrown down the corridor, only when I went to see what it was I could find no spoon and no explanation for the noise'.

Another incident was recorded on her mobile phone's video facility, again while she was in the flat on her own:

> I woke up one night to the sound of a banging noise in my room: one minute it was in my room, the next it was coming from out in the corridor. It was really terrifying and I knew no one would believe me so I grabbed my mobile and recorded the noises. I successfully taped them but on the recording they are not as clear as they were on the actual night.

By far the most spectacular account of her uninvited guest came when I asked her if she or any of her flatmates had seen anything move around with their own eyes:

> You know, there was one thing I meant to tell you, and you have just reminded me about it. My flatmate, Rosie, went in to her room one night and to her utter horror she saw a bottle of water standing on its edge on a table top, leaning over 45 degrees and spinning on the spot. Round and round it went; she couldn't believe her eyes and was rooted to the spot.

In all honesty, I couldn't believe what I was hearing. I asked Gemma if she was having me on and she said 'most certainly not' – and I truly believe her. On a poltergeist case I investigated in 2006, fellow investigator Mike Hallowell and I actually recorded this phenomenon on videotape at a house in South Shields; a bottle balancing on its edge of its own volition, although it was not spinning round as in Rosie's case. Nevertheless, the same phenomenon had occurred in our investigation. We know this is exactly the type of pointless things that poltergeists can do – why is another question!

This led me to believe Gemma and her flatmates may have been experiencing a low-level poltergeist infestation. I arranged a time to visit Gemma in her home, as more investigation was needed and some experiments of my own were now required to see if I could catch anything paranormal on tape. On Monday 2 June 2008, Mike Hallowell and I arrived at the flat at about 12.30 p.m. We were met by Gemma and one of her flatmates, Liz Mills; another housemate, Jo Risolino, was at the shop getting in some supplies for our visit. She soon arrived home and after a cup of tea the girls regaled us with some more stories of the ghostly goings-on by the phantom they had nicknamed 'Tom'.

Jo started first. She told us that one night she woke up to find a dark shadow in her room, and to her horror realised it was standing over her bed. In fact, the night before our visit she experienced what she described as 'a creeping, ice-cold rush that began at my toes and crept right over my body; then, as quick as it came, it went'. Gemma went on to tell us that she had recently heard footsteps walking along the narrow corridor while she was in her bedroom; they ceased after they reached half way. We were then informed that Rosie, although not present on our visit that day, had experienced her television being turned on in her room when no one else was around. Liz Mills had experienced nothing to date, but that was soon to change.

During the afternoon we spent there we carried out a number of tests and experiments, but little did we know how successful we were to be. We recorded knocks

The Bigg Market in 1820. (Courtesy of Newcastle Libraries and Information Service)

and bumps coming from Gemma's room which sounded like something was clattering around in there. An incredible long, drawn-out breath was heard by all present, which drove the girls wild with excitement – and fear. Finally, a 6ft three-dimensional black shadow was seen by all five of us while we investigated the passageway. This was Liz's first experience of paranormal activity at her home, and, deep down, I don't think she liked it! A date for a full investigation was then planned in which we would put the flat under twenty-four hour surveillance with CCTV, video cameras and all the latest mod-cons in the hope that maybe we could catch 'Tom' on tape. The results of that investigation can be found at the back of this book.

Ewan McDonald

From inside buildings in the Bigg Market to outside in the Bigg Market itself. A number of stories persist regarding a haunting in this vicinity, although they differ in some ways. Many years ago, in the eighteenth century, it was believed that a brutal murder took place here. A local man was beaten to death after taunting a Scotsman, Ewan McDonald, who was wearing a kilt. Subsequently, Ewan was hanged by his neck from the gallows for his brutal act and it is his ghost that is said to haunt the Bigg Market.

One version says that his ghost is regularly seen inside the pub once known as the Pig and Whistle, standing out of place in an otherwise busy city-centre bar, while other stories suggest that his ghost is seen wondering around the cobbles further up the Bigg market, perhaps haunting the scene of his crime. I have even heard that the ghost of Ewan McDonald has been seen in the gent's public loos situated in the Bigg market opposite the Bee Hive pub.

Whatever the truth, the ghost of Ewan has not been seen for many years now, although the Bigg Market quite often sees men wearing kilts, usually frequenting the many pubs the Bigg Market is famous for. Alas, it is not the ghost of Ewan, but groups of partygoers visiting from over the borders – or merely just the fun-loving Geordies dressed up for a 'mad neet oot'.

Disturbances at the Dental Hospital

The Dental Hospital in the Spital Tongues area of the city was said to be the home of a ghost. This phantom is one of Newcastle's more famous ghosts, although the building is relatively new in comparison to others in Newcastle. It was built around 1977, and the hauntings seemed to have occurred during the 1980s and '90s as the medical staff reported unexplained happenings at the time.

The resident spectre was said to be a helpful ghost. On occasion the staff would find the dental tools and instruments set out in the morning after they had been cleaned and put away for the night.

Another account says that one witness at the time was working in the hospital and was tending to his duties. As he made his way down one of long corridors he suddenly became aware of a presence. Footsteps – but not his – were heard coming down the corridor behind him as he made his way down the passageway. He turned and looked, but no one could be seen. An immediate search of the rooms proved fruitless as no one, at least from our realm, could be found.

Another account comes from a member of staff who was working at the hospital during twilight. This witness also heard the phantom footsteps, only on this occasion they came from the floor above. As you can imagine, being in the hospital at night with nothing but the deathly silence enveloping you would be an eerie prospect to begin with. The footsteps would have reverberated around the corridors and been amplified by the echoic conditions; enough to send shivers down the spine. Of course, the thought occurred that an intruder was in the premises, but an inspection found this was not the case. I don't think any explanations were ever put forward as to what the disturbances were, but from my perspective it seems that a very low-level poltergeist infestation may have been the cause. True, it went on longer than most poltergeists do with intermittent outbursts of activity, but it can't be ruled out. A further thought occurs that it could well have been a caring old ghost of someone who liked to lend a hand.

The Pink Lady of Jesmond Towers

On 27 March 2008, a local newspaper printed an article relaying the sad news that the La Sagesse School for girls was expected to close in the summer of 2008 due to falling numbers of pupils (combined with the soaring rental costs). It went on to say that the £3,000-a-term school in the Jesmond area of the city would close, leaving over 200 pupils looking for a new school and over fifty staff unemployed. The school is incorporated into Jesmond Towers (formally known as West Jesmond House), which is an elaborate gothic-style Grade II listed building and was once the home of North-East shipbuilder Charles Mitchell. Not only is Jesmond Towers (La Sagesse School) well known in the region for its beautiful architecture and wonderful history, but it is also known to be the home of a ghost referred to as the Pink Lady. Reports of this spectral visitor have been documented time and time again over the years, although nowadays the ghost is said to be that of a White Lady.

This common characteristic intrigues me to say the least, and there may indeed be a theory as to what is going on there. They say apparitions can eventually die away after haunting a certain area for many years, and it seems quite likely that this is the case at Jesmond Towers. In the early days of the ghost sighting, this phantom was seen wearing a red dress; over time she became known as the Pink Lady, and it seems now she is seen in white. My guess is that in 100 or so years nothing more than her faint outline will be observed – or merely the sound of her footfalls or dress rustling as she walks by. Her ghost has been seen in the school on many occasions. She appears in the classrooms and along the corridors, and then she disappears without a trace – leaving the witnesses, normally the schoolgirls, quite shaken up. She has also been seen on a narrow stairwell that leads to the roof.

The phantom is thought to be that of an Emily Cooke, who resided here in around 1890. She was a guest at Jesmond Towers after being widowed and, as you can imagine, her health was not quite as it should have been. Some might have said that 'she was in the depths of despair'. It is said that early one morning she silently made her way up a narrow stairwell that led to the top of the towers, where she proceeded to throw herself from the top. She would have fallen about 60ft before hitting the ground, which resulted in her instantaneous death. Could the stairwell where she has been observed in recent times be the same stairwell she took to end her miserable life?

The Hooded Wraith of Blandford Street Museum

During the course of my research I decided to enlist the help of my good friend Mike Hallowell. Mike writes the WraithScape column in his local newspaper *The Shields Gazette*, and has done so for over ten years. He is no stranger to the paranormal; indeed, it was Mike Hallowell who I called in to assist me with a poltergeist case that occurred in 2006, resulting in the pair of us writing an enormous tome detailing the whole affair. As a columnist, Mike gets inundated with e-mails and letters from his readers telling him about their 'spooky stories'. I asked Mike if he would let me look through his files and, like the true gentleman he is, he duly obliged. What follows is an account that I managed to dig out of Mike's archives and, with his kind permission, I have reproduced it here.

A reader called Dorothy relayed a terrifying experience that she had several years ago whilst visiting a library in Newcastle. 'I was deeply into my family tree', Dorothy states, 'but was stuck on one member. My husband Stan and myself decided to go to Newcastle Museum, in Blandford Street, as some records were held there'.

They travelled to Newcastle one bitterly cold morning in January, with high hopes of finding the information they required. They entered the room where the microfiche machines were kept, and Stan sat down in front of the number three viewer. Dorothy, meanwhile, sat at a large table with a huge pile of books. She remembers feeling the pleasant warmth of the winter sun on her back as it streamed through the library window.

As time passed the sun shifted position, and, as a consequence, so did Dorothy. She moved to another table, which was now bathed in sunlight. Several times Dorothy's eyes were drawn to a set of filing cabinets in the corner. She kept getting fleeting glimpses of something moving, but whenever she looked directly towards the cabinets the movement stopped. Then she caught another movement out of the corner of her eye, but this was nothing like the first.

'I got the shock of my life', she says.

> Floating over the filing cabinets was what looked like a hooded monk, but the face was just a skull. It had eyes, though. It was horrible and I was scared, but I couldn't stop watching it. It suddenly disappeared, but the room felt very cold. Somehow I felt it was still there, watching me, even though I couldn't see it.

Dorothy didn't tell her husband immediately, but decided to go and sit next to him for some moral support. As she did so, another chap jumped up from his microfiche viewer and ran out of the room as fast as his legs could carry him. Had he seen the hooded skull too? That was enough for Dorothy. She decided to leave her husband to his own research and vacate the premises as quickly as possible.

On the way out Dorothy decided to visit the ladies' powder room. She switched on the light and walked towards the first cubicle, the door of which was composed of wooden louver slats. Suddenly, Dorothy felt the same presence as she had in the library. She peered through the slats, and was horrified to see the same hooded skull staring at her intently.

Dorothy turned her head away and found herself looking at the mirror on the powder-room wall. She noticed that the strange, disembodied skull had no reflection. Without further delay, she switched off the light and left the premises as quickly as possible.

Dorothy is philosophical about her experience, although she is totally at a loss to explain it. 'Some of my friends believe me, others don't,' she says, 'but it doesn't bother me because I know its true'.

Now it would be easy just to dismiss Dorothy's story as the product of an over-excited imagination. After all, even by paranormal standards her story is unusual to say

An artist's impression of an evil, grinning, hooded figure that was allegedly seen in the Blandford Museum. (Illustration by Julie Olley)

the least, but there may be more to this story than meets the eye. Other people have also mentioned that they too have had similar experiences to Dorothy in the very same place.

Shop 17, Old Vickers Yard – Elswick

Vickers Yard at Elswick has provided employment for local people for many years now. What many people do not know, however, is that the yard also played host to a ghost. The story begins back in the early 1930s when a foreman at the yard named Freddie Bolam found himself in a degree of domestic bother. Details are vague, but it seems the hope of a romantic relationship had recently turned sour. A newspaper at the time reported quite tactfully that he had been 'let down in love'.

Sadly, it seemed that Freddie's life was no longer worth living and he committed suicide. His body was never found, but his clothes were discovered piled neatly on the banks of the Tyne. Everyone who knew Freddie was convinced he had thrown himself into the river while in this deep state of depression.

Freddie, who was known for wearing his bowler hat, was responsible for looking after a manufacturing unit called Shop 17. Over a decade after his death, workers in Shop 17 began to see flitting shadows move around the place with no obvious cause. Subsequently a large number of workers asked for a transfer to other parts of the yard.

One evening, a security guard in Shop 17 felt a hand touch him upon the shoulder and it seemed to hold him back with a force. When he turned around to see who was there he was surprised to be greeted by no one at all. Not long after this episode, two fitters claimed to have had a long conversation with Freddie, although they had no idea whom he was or that he was dead. After viewing old pictures of Freddie the Foreman, they identified him as the man they had spoken to.

Eventually Shop 17 closed down; however, in 1974 it was reopened. Once again the ghost of Freddie Bolam began to make his presence known. There was a crane situated over Shop 17 and a number of crane operatives testified that they could 'sense something' inside the operator's cab that troubled them deeply. More than one operative refused to use that crane again.

On 21 November 1975, one cab operative arrived at Shop 17 for his night shift but before he began his work in the crane his attention was drawn to a man wearing an old-fashioned suit with a bowler hat. The thought occurs that it could have been Freddie Bolam's ghost making his presence felt once more. Not sure what to do, the worker approached the figure and began a conversation with him. We are not too sure what the conversation was about, but nevertheless it was cut short as the operative had to begin his shift.

He began to climb up the crane ladders to the cab when he happened to glance back at where the mysterious visitor had been standing: to his surprise, he had completely vanished. The view from his position on the ladder led him to think that this was very odd as there was no way the man in the suit could have walked out of sight in such a short time. His view of the yard was almost panoramic.

Puzzled, he climbed up into his cab and prepared himself to sit in the cab seat. Just as he was about to sit down, when, to his horror, he was grabbed from behind by a pair of unseen hands and literally thrown across the empty cab. Worse, it soon became obvious to the worker that whatever was in there with him was trying to kill him, as it attempted to drag him across the cab and throw him to his death from the cab door!

A struggle ensued, after which he managed to free himself and clamber down the ladders to the safety of the ground – whereupon he immediately quit his job, never to return. Newspaper reports at the time said that the cab operative was convinced that the entity that besieged him was none other than Freddie the Foreman, but my colleague Mike Hallowell, from whom I gleaned this fascinating story, is not so sure. He thinks that the driver was attacked by something a lot more sinister than a ghost, as ghosts are not usually prone to committing vicious attacks. He thinks that Freddie may well have been trying to warn him of the impending danger, and I for one agree.

Ghost Girl on the Wall – Denton

A few years ago I received a letter from a lady called Jenny telling me about a strange experience she had in 1992 while carrying out a school project on Hadrian's Wall in the Denton Burn area of the city. She had seen a published article I had written on ghosts and decided to tell me her story.

A small section of Hadrian's Wall stretching about 30ft is still in existence in this area, which is on the outskirts of Newcastle city centre. It was here that she and her friend experienced something rather strange.

During the course of their visit they were looking at the wall, taking measurements and generally researching their project. It was a nice summer's morning and the sun was bathing the girls in a warm and soothing light. Suddenly, the area around them went rather cold and they became aware that they were not alone. They could see no one to account for this feeling, and so they thought nothing about it and proceeded with their work. A few photographs of the remains of the wall were taken at the time as part of their project; after a few hours of work, they called it a day.

A few days went by and the photographs that had been taken on the day were due to be picked up, as processing back in those days was not as prompt as it is today. The pictures were collected and viewed by the girls. Nothing seemed to be amiss until Jenny noticed the figure of a young girl standing in one of the frames near the wall. In Jenny's words:

> I went to take pictures of the wall with my friend for our project, and there was no one else around, but when we had the photos developed one of them had a picture of a young girl standing by the wall. It was a slightly hazy outline, but perfectly formed. I can't really remember the period of her clothing or anything as it was a long time ago. All that I can remember is, it was a little girl, and we could see from her thighs upwards so the wall must have been blocking her legs from the knees down. She was just standing there. She had long hair and if I remember correctly she had a long dress on.

I contacted Jenny and asked if I could see the picture, but I was told it had been lost sometime during the preceding years. (At least, Jenny presumed it was long gone.) She did tell me that the picture could still be in the loft with all of the other junk that is usually stored up in loft spaces and if ever she cleaned it out, a search would be undertaken to find the picture. To this day no photograph has materialised, but you never know – we live in hope!

A few things strike me about this account. The first is that, due to the sense they were not alone, the girls looked around before the pictures were taken, which indicates that there was almost certainly no one else around when the image was taken. The second thing is the fact that the surrounding air went cold prior to the pictures being taken. Had the sun disappeared behind a cloud for a fleeting moment? Or, as in most supernatural experiences, did the temperature drop due to a paranormal presence? I guess we will never know for sure, but one thing is certain – the girls are convinced they once photographed a ghost of a girl standing next to Hadrian's Wall.

The section of Hadrian's Wall at Denton Burn where a strange image was captured.

Interestingly, during my research for this book, I came across a story regarding the ghost of Denton Hall (which stands over the road from this stretch of Hadrian's Wall) and was astonished to find out that not only has the hall a ghost of an old lady but there are rumours of a murder that took place there too. It was believed by villagers and locals – though it couldn't be proved – that a jealous woman murdered her younger sister for reasons no one can specify, and her restless ghost is said to wander the hall and the surrounding area. If true, and one day the story can be verified, it would be a tantalising notion to suggest that the ghost girl photographed near the wall by Jenny and her friend could well be the ghost of the murdered girl from West Denton Hall.

Denton Hall

It is a little-known fact that Denton Hall was built on the site where the monks of Tynemouth Priory once resided. It is a manor with Elizabethan-style architecture and stands majestically surrounded by tall trees on the Newcastle to Carlisle Road. The hall has been in the hands of the clergy for many years now and, at the time of writing, is home to the Bishop of Hexham and Newcastle. The resident ghost at this particular abode is very well known among the local Denton folk, as it is in all of Newcastle too.

Denton Hall, a beautiful old manor house haunted by a ghost known locally as 'Old Barbery'. The ghost of a young girl who was reputedly murdered is also said to reside there.

As previously mentioned, the alleged tale of a murdered girl is attached to this building and it was believed that she was strangled here on these premises. But it is not the murdered girl that is famous for haunting the hall. No – that privilege goes to the old woman with grey hair known as 'Old Barbery' or 'Silky'. Said to be a kind and compassionate spectre, Old Barbery walks the corridors and rooms of Denton Hall, although there are two rooms that she is said to specifically inhabit.

One of the more unadulterated accounts of the ghost of Denton Hall comes from a female guest who was staying there after she had attended a dance in Newcastle city centre. She was sitting in a wooden chair getting ready for her bed when she happened to look up. To her surprise she saw, sitting in the other wooden chair, a woman that was dressed in an old-fashioned flowered satin gown which bore a decorated triangular panel that filled in the aperture of a lady's gown known as a stomacher. She wore large rings on her fingers and an odd-shaped hood over her head which obscured part of her old, wrinkled face. No sooner had the phantom been spotted, she disappeared, leaving behind the sound of her rustling dress in her wake as though she had stood up and walked out of the room. The startled guest then rushed to the door to find it was locked, and she remembered she had locked it herself upon entering.

Other accounts have been reported too, and on one occasion Old Barbery was seen to grasp the hand of a sleeping person. This resulted in the skin of the sleeper being very tender and sore where the apparition had touched it. Old Barbery has also been

Denton Hall in 1900. (Courtesy of Newcastle Libraries and Information Service)

spotted outside in the hall's grounds walking silently under the trees and along the pathways. Nowadays she makes her presence known in different ways. Knocks, bumps and thumps are heard in the house, along with the sound of something being dragged from room to room. The last documented occurrence was when a window on the stairwell landing was thrown open with considerable force. Interestingly, on a recent visit to take photographs of the hall a nice old Denton local approached me after she had noticed what I was doing. She went on to tell me that as a local resident of the area she knew quite a bit regarding this 'beautiful old building', as she called it, and subsequently told me all about it. She even mentioned it was allegedly haunted, so I asked her if she knew anything in regards to the ghost.

> The hall was originally owned by the Montague family who also owned the old pit that was once in operation nearby. The family had a butler that worked there, and rumours circulating at the time indicated that it was he that murdered – by strangulation – the girl that is said to

haunt the building. After discovering she knew the whereabouts of some family treasure that was buried – or a priceless artifact – he attempted to force the information from her in a violent way by strangling her with her own long hair. He went a little too far, resulting in the woman's death. It is her ghost that is said to haunt the building and grounds.

An interesting account to say the least, and, as you may have noticed, it differs slightly from the other account mentioned earlier in this section; but the fact remains that this happens with some ghost accounts. They do get altered; facts can become fiction, and little pieces of story become inadvertently added to the narrative to the point where it is impossible to separate the real facts from fiction. Whatever the truth behind the murder at Denton Hall, the reality remains that the sightings of a female ghost and unexplained noises have been reported over the years, leaving me in no doubt that the building is haunted.

One final thought occurs: perhaps, if the little old lady I spoke to was correct with her version, the ghost shows herself for a reason, perhaps in an effort to reveal the whereabouts of the hidden treasure?

The Lemington Man in Black

The district of Lemington is about two miles west of Newcastle city centre, and it was here, in Maud Street back in 1974, that an unwelcome guest began to appear in the house of a young woman. It all began one night when she retired to bed and was woken up during the night by a figure standing by her bed. At first she felt as though she was being watched while in the bedroom. When she sat up to take a look, there he was, bold as brass, looking at her. He was standing by the fireplace with a stern expression upon his gaunt face. He had black hair, and was wearing a shirt with an outdated collar and a long, black coat.

Putting this down to imagination, she went back to sleep and thought nothing more about it. Three months later the man in black appeared in her room once more. This time she was convinced it was a ghost. After that, more odd occurrences were reported at the house. Her eight-year-old daughter was violently thrown out of bed one night, while on another occasion one of the armchairs in the house suddenly burst into flames for no apparent reason. Other terrifying phenomena were reported too, with the pages of a book being turned as if by invisible fingers – while the book was actually being read – and mirrors on the walls breaking and falling to the floor.

The disturbances at the Maud Street house continued until one day the woman of the house was rushed to hospital as she could take no more. A nervous breakdown ensued and a relative subsequently looked after the children. A local priest was then called in to help and subsequently 'blessed the house'. This seemed to have done the trick, but the family in question was still frightened witless and requested to be rehoused. The local housing association took her complaints very seriously and helped the family to move.

An artist's impression of the Lemington man in black standing next to a woman in bed. (Illustration by Julie Olley)

This account made the local newspapers back in December 1974, and it is from an old clipping that I found in Mike Hallowell's archives I was able to gain access to this terrifying account. In the newspaper the family are named and a photograph of the woman and one of her daughters accompanies the article. I have chosen to keep the family anonymous, although the locale in this account is correct.

The Ghosts of Hawthorn Leslie's

Hawthorn Leslie's had two sites in Newcastle upon Tyne. One was near Forth Banks in town, in which Robert Hawthorn had founded the complex in 1817, and the other in Low Walker, where the beautiful St Peter's Basin is now located. This complex was founded in 1884 and both sites were reputed to be haunted. Hawthorn Leslie's was one of the North East's most eminent industrial corporations in Newcastle, and in 1884 it began to specialise in manufacturing two types of commodity. The famous shipbuilder A. Leslie & Co. joined forces with Robert & W. Hawthorn, which was already a renowned manufacturer of locomotion parts, and together they amalgamated into one manufacturing business – thus forming Hawthorn Leslie.

The haunted building at the Forth Banks complex was actually called Forth Banks House, and psychic disturbances occurred here on a regular basis, so it seems. Every night the alarms would mysteriously go off by themselves for no known reason and they always went off during the night. The poor chap who was on call could never find signs of intruders or even an attempt at a break in. The electrics were checked over and found to be in perfect working order. One night a vigil was carried out to see if a conclusion could be drawn as to why the alarms kept activating.

A few employees locked themselves in and waited. Sure enough, the alarms were tripped, but no one was found at all inside the building, although the sounds of footfalls could be heard walking through the corridors – ultimately setting off the other alarms in the process. This confused the investigators, as all the doors to each corridor were locked and bolted. It seems that whatever was setting off the alarms must have been moving through the doors. There was no other explanation for what happened that night.

My father was an employee of Hawthorn Leslie's for twenty years and worked at the St Peter's complex from 1961–1981 (when he was sadly made redundant). The factory stood for a number of years before its eventual demolition in the mid-1980s. My childhood home was literally a stone's throw away from the complex and after a short meander down the Cherry Walk you would be there. During the period when

Hawthorn Leslie's factory at St Peter's; the site of many strange occurrences.

A modern view of the aforementioned picture, now St Peter's Marina.

The derelict Copper Shop at Hawthorn Leslie's, one of the areas where the ghost was seen. (Courtesy of Walter Ritson)

My father takes a tea break in the copper shop during his employment at the factory. (Courtesy of Walter Ritson)

the factory lay derelict I would often venture down there and play in the old factory buildings, generally getting up to mischief. Little did I know I was playing in a haunted place! My father informed me that there was an area named the Copper Shop in this particular complex that was known for its paranormal activity. Many reports came in of a man who was seen next to the door wearing old-style clothing and a bowler hat. The ghost often moved silently around before vanishing into thin air, yet the strange thing was that most of the sightings began at the door.

Believed to be the ghost of an ex-foreman, this phantom would be seen in and around the Copper Shop during working hours and at night. As a child I remember my father coming home from work and telling mother about the latest sightings of 'the man in a bowler hat'. I asked my father if he had ever seen the ghost during his twenty years working there, and he informed me that he never had, although the Copper Shop was not his actual work area. He told me many of his work colleagues did see the ghost and were terrified of it, with some witnesses refusing to enter the workshop alone. My father was, and still is, a photographer, and he once attempted to photograph the ghost by taking a series of snaps in the Copper Shop (unfortunately to no avail). One of those pictures of the derelict Copper Shop is reproduced in this book.

This story bears a striking resemblance to the 'Freddy the Foreman' tale at the old Vickers Yard in Elswick which featured earlier in this book. He too wears a bowler hat and is seen in old clothing. During my research and the compilation of this book

I presumed someone might have had their wires crossed somewhere and had maybe become mixed up. Or perhaps there were two versions of this particular ghost story? Then I found out that in the late 1800s and early 1900s all the foremen wore the same attire: a suit and a bowler hat! Perhaps no mix-up occurred at all, so one wonders just how many more phantom foremen in old suits and bowler hats there are haunting the modern-day municipality.

The Unknown Ghost of Hadrian's Way

Hadrian's Way is a stretch of path that leads from Wallsend to Newcastle upon Tyne and was once used as a railway line. The area has long been reputed to be haunted and as a child growing up I often used to hear the stories of the phantoms that resided down by the old 'Cherry Walk', as it was once known. My father had had his own experience when he saw the ghost of a young boy playing out on the railway late at night. He watched attentively as the figure of the young lad disappeared in front of his very eyes. This next account is my own, and occurred one day many years ago while I was out playing with my friends.

I was in the grounds of the old Hawthorn Leslie's factory (now St Peter's Basin) when I realised it was time to go home. I said goodbye to my friends and told them I might see them later. I then started to climb up the steep grass embankment and fought my way through the trees and bushes until I reached the railway line next to Shepherd's scrap yard.

As I was walking home along the railway line, I suddenly became aware of someone behind me and I felt that he or she was following me. I suspected this as I heard their footsteps right behind me crunching along on the gravel. I then turned around to see who it was, and to my surprise there was no one there.

Now, I knew the footsteps were right behind me, and no one could have hidden in the time it took me to turn around and look. I stopped, had a quick look around, thought for a moment and then resumed my short journey home. Immediately, as I started to stroll along again, I heard the footsteps – only this time they sounded even closer than before. I turned around again – this time starting to panic a little – and still there was no one there. I then ran home as fast as I could.

The Phantom Jogger of Armstrong Park

Armstrong Park is a beautiful area of parkland that is situated in the east end of Newcastle upon Tyne. It is approximately one and a half miles from the city centre and is a very popular area for walking, cycling, and visiting in general. In times gone by, Armstrong Park was mistaken for other parks, as there are a few really close by – namely Heaton Park, and Jesmond Dene. At one time they were all collectively known as one or the other. Some classed them all as Heaton Park, some Armstrong Park and others Jesmond Dene.

The old railway line, now known as Hadrian's Way, where the author heard strange footsteps and felt as though he was being followed.

Lord Armstrong – the English industrialist and engineer – donated the land that is now Armstrong Park to the city in 1883, and there was some misunderstanding as to what park(s) would be known as. The council then decided to separate these parks by roads and lanes for clarity and since then there has been no mistaking the difference between the three.

On many a crisp and cold autumn day I have meandered my way through the desolate, often lonely pathways that festoon these serene and wonderful areas of natural beauty. It never occurred to me that those paths, intertwining through miles of dense forests and woodland, could be haunted. I don't know why; it just didn't. The clues are there; old desolate ruins can be found in all three parks, buildings that obviously date back hundreds of years – the famous old water mill in Jesmond Dene, now a Grade II listed building, and the wonderful old twelfth-century ruin that once was St Mary's Chapel, among others. In Heaton Park there is an old shell of a ruin with only two sides left standing and a wonderful arched doorway leading into what may have been the old Heaton Hall.

In Armstrong Park there is an old tower that stands majestically on a small mound of land overlooking the tennis courts and bowling greens in the east and the city centre. They are obscured by the trees, and behind those trees there is an old pathway that runs through the park situated down by the wooded embankment. It is this path that I now wish to elaborate on. This ghost story was relayed to me a few years ago now, and it is one haunting that has never been documented in a book of this kind (although according to witnesses it did feature in the local newspapers).

Old Mill at Jesmond Dene.

The individual that passed on the story to me is an honest, reliable gentleman with a sensible head on his shoulders. I know this for a fact because the man who saw the ghost in Armstrong Park was my own father. Here is his story, in his own words:

> One Tuesday night in September 1986, on the way home from Shiremoor, the Metro train I was on broke down and we had to wait for the replacement bus service. Since the train had come to a standstill at Jesmond Metro Station and I was in close vicinity to Jesmond Dene, I decided to walk and pick up my bus at Heaton instead ... It was not far to walk, so I headed off on my short journey (which took me past the River Ouseburn, into Armstrong Park and onto the path down from the old tower). It was getting dark by this time and I was in a hurry to get out at the other end where Armstrong Park joins Heaton Park.
>
> As I continued along the path, a figure ran past me from behind. He was tall, thin and in silhouette due to the light levels being so poor. It was not until the runner had gone by that I realised he had made no noises whatsoever: no footfalls, no heavy breathing, nothing. I also thought it was strange how he was so tall.
>
> After that I thought nothing more of it, until about 12 months later when I read about someone else's account in a newspaper concerning a ghost story in and around the same area. When I heard that that stretch of pathway was allegedly haunted, it brought all my memories back to me from that night. The story I heard concerned a phantom runner, who was seen in shadow form, and ran along 12in above the ground.

The lonely path that runs through Armstrong Park where the 'phantom jogger' has been seen on a number of occasions.

A Haunted Hotel in Jesmond

'Staff Spooked by Hotel Ghost.' That was the headline in a local paper after reports of strange goings-on were experienced in a hotel in the Jesmond area of the city. The disturbances happened many, many years ago, and recent enquiries have proved the haunting has ceased. Because of the requested anonymity, I shall make it my business to refrain from revealing the name of this particular venue due to the many 'unwanted ghost-hunting teams' that will no doubt make their own enquires and request overnight vigils. The haunting is finished, however, the story is still an interesting one so the details – and the details only – of this previously spooky guest house shall be told once more.

During the height of the disturbances the hotel staff were scared at the thought of their ethereal visitor, although the phantom was quite harmless. Strange things would take place at the hotel, including the disappearance and then sudden reappearance of certain objects that belonged to guests. On one occasion a woman went to sleep wearing her watch and woke up the following morning to find it had gone. She looked in her bed, under her bed; in fact she almost tore the room to pieces in search of it, but to no avail. She had almost given up on finding it when, out of the blue, it turned up in a location she had already searched – typically mischievous activity put down to playful but harmless spirits.

A friend of the (then) manager reported seeing a phantom receptionist sitting behind the counter in the lobby when she knew no one was in. The hotel at that time did not have twenty-four hour service like it does today and the staff had vacated the premises or retired to their rooms at about 11 p.m. The woman, 'dressed in a black-polo neck jumper and sporting a page-boy haircut', was seen at 11.30 p.m. and was not recognised by the witness. A second glance, moments later, proved even stranger – the mystery woman had disappeared altogether! A search followed, but no one of that description was found. Other occurrences included a brooch which vanished without a trace from a guest's bedroom and turned up elsewhere in the hotel. Also, a contraption on a kitchen wall which was used to hold paper was found to be empty: the paper that was previously attached to it was scattered all over the floor.

Some staff did not take the disturbances seriously and attempts at rational explanations were put forward. One lady who had worked there for a few years said, 'Some of the staff get very scared talking about it but as far as I am concerned there is nothing to it.' Another opinion expressed was; 'I suppose there are things that happen everywhere which leave behind a mystery. It's all too easy to put it down to something like a ghost.' The best quote from this case came from the (then) manager, who simply said, 'Ghosts can be a convenient excuse for an unsolved incident.' Quite true: I have to agree there that a lot of alleged hauntings usually do have rational explanations and if one is convinced of a haunting, every sound heard, every seemingly strange occurrence can, and often does, get misinterpreted as paranormal phenomena.

There are, however, people who are convinced the hotel was indeed haunted. The witness that saw the phantom receptionist behind the counter was convinced that the visitor was otherworldly and states, 'I know what I saw'. I guess the lady who lost her watch through the night was also pretty dumbfounded. It also became apparent that a member of staff – a chambermaid – was accidentally gassed to death in one of the rooms in the 1940s, so it could be her restless spirit that wanders around the hotel pinching people's belongings and generally getting up to no good.

The Haunting of Willington Mill

The poltergeist at Willington Millhouse is by far the most famous and well-attested haunting that this area of Tyneside has ever seen. The village of Willington Quay lies to the east of the city centre approximately five miles along the River Tyne. Old books and older Ordnance Survey maps record Willington Quay as either Newcastle or near Newcastle, but nowadays the area is better known as Tyne and Wear. Although Willington Mill is not strictly Newcastle upon Tyne these days, I do feel the story warrants inclusion in the volume – after all, it is on the border.

Meticulously documented in the archives of the Society for Psychical Research (SPR) and written up in great detail in Harry Price's magnificent 1945 tome *Poltergeist Over England*, the haunting of Willington Mill began in 1835 and persisted for twelve years. It eventually ceased in 1847, which is remarkable as usually poltergeist infestations (as this was believed to be) normally last only a few months.

Mr Edmund Procter and his father, Joseph Procter, a well-respected and religious man, owned the haunted house at this time. These were the key witnesses to the bizarre array of bewildering phenomena – which included a ghostly lady who smelt of lavender, doors opening and closing on their own, the sound of furniture being dragged across the floors in empty rooms (this kept the Procters awake at night for years), unexplained ghastly smells, and the classic poltergeist manifestation of thunderous bangs and raps emanating from nowhere.

A woman with no eyes in her sockets was also seen in the upper bedrooms of the house by two amateur ghost sleuths who were staking out the room at the time of the hauntings. One passed out with fright – and when he came around, they both fled in fear! If you think that was strange, then what happened next was even stranger: a variety of ghost animals began to appear in the house! (These comprised of a cat and a monkey.) After twelve years the hauntings seemed to stop, but by then the Procters had relocated to North Shields. Harry Price reproduces some of the detailed dairy extracts taken from the case, and they make fabulous reading. He also states, quite correctly, that:

> The case is very important for several reasons. The account has been prepared from the contemporary diary kept by the chief witness, Mr Joseph Procter, who was a god-fearing man and a well-known Quaker. Very few poltergeist cases are so fully documented, and fewer still are the contemporary diaries, by responsible persons, that can be brought in as evidence. There are day-to-day diaries relating to the disturbances at Borley Rectory, Ballechin House, the 'Mill on the Eden' and one or two more good cases, but such invaluable records are of rare occurrence.
>
> In order to leave to posterity an authentic account, Edmund Procter sent his father's diaries to the Society for Psychical Research for publication. They appear in the *SPR Journal*, Vol. V, 1891-92, pp. 331-352.

The site of Willington Millhouse, one of the North's most well-attested cases of poltergeist activity.

One of the site warehouses that stood adjacent to the haunted Millhouse. It still stands after almost 200 years.

Bringing it up to date, a factory now occupies the site of the one-time haunted mill house and one of the original warehouses that stood adjacent to the building is still there to this day. It's interesting to note that Price states there are very few poltergeist cases that are documented with day-to-day diaries, making these particular cases so essential in an evidential respect. Since the Willington Mill days there have been a number of documented poltergeist cases, some very interesting indeed, but not on this level.

There are, however, two recent poltergeist cases that spring to mind that can compare in respect to the length of infestation, the intensity of the phenomena, and of course its documentation: the Enfield Poltergeist (1977-78), investigated by the late Maurice Grosse and my (now) fellow associate Guy Lyon Playfair, and the South Shields poltergeist (2005-06) that I investigated with fellow researcher Mike Hallowell. Both of these cases also have meticulous day-to-day dairies written by those that witnessed the phenomena, as well as the notes of the investigators. Both cases are documented in the SPR archives and are vital to the progression of poltergeist research.

The Plaguey Field (Grannies Park) and the Ouseburn Board School

Known locally as Grannies Park, and once known as the Plaguey Field due to the mass burials of plague victims, this small area of land tucked away behind the old Ouseburn Board School is allegedly haunted. It is said that a few suicides have taken place around this area (one in the field itself, and the other inside the school). Rumour has it that a former headmaster of the Ouseburn Board School took himself into the field one day and hanged himself from a tree. His ghost is said to haunt the area of land where he took his life.

Local rumour claims that on occasion his sad spectre can be seen standing under the tree where his life ended. I heard another story that suggests the ghost of his lifeless corpse has been seen hanging from the tree, swaying from side to side in the gentle breeze – though in the blink of an eye, it's gone. A very disturbing echo from the past, to say the least! It is also said that restless spirits of the victims of the plague still walk the area in which they are buried.

The other ghost is said to haunt the tower block in the nearby Ouseburn Board School – also believed to be the place where another hanging took place. This time the depressed individual was one of the schoolteachers. His wandering spectre is said to been seen on the stairwell in the tower block. It is thought that if you encounter his pathetic wraith bad luck will befall you. The school is a Grade II listed building and was built around 1893. However, due to unforeseen circumstances which were beyond the control of the local authorities it was closed in the 1960s. It is now used as a business development centre by the council and has been since it reopened in the early 1990s. The ghost, incidentally, has not been seen for some years, much to the relief of the staff that presently work there.

A path of graves runs through the 'Plaguey Field' at Byker. It is said to be haunted by the ghost of an old teacher from nearby Ouseburn Board School who hung himself in the trees.

An artist's impression of the dead man hanging from the trees in the Plaguey Field. (Illustration by Julie Olley)

The Lost Birds of Jesmond Dene

Earlier in the book I took the reader to Armstrong Park, one of three public parks and areas of natural beauty that are in this region of Newcastle. (It is also where the phantom jogger is said to run.) We now go back to this wonderful area of the city where we shall visit Jesmond Dene and learn about the ghost birds that are said to reside there. To be honest, I had never actually heard of 'the ghost birds of Jesmond Dene' until I read a book called *Mystery Animals of Northumberland and Tyneside*. Published by the Centre for Fortean Zoology (CFZ), and written by my good friend Mike Hallowell, this book takes a look at Fortean phenomena that are associated with the area.

After reading the chapter based on these birds I immediately telephoned Mike and asked him if I could reproduce some sections of his book herein as I felt that it was not only a good story but also a good ghost account that fits in with the criteria of this book. It is also a story that brings back memories from years ago – memories I will never forget. You see, as a boy I was a keen ornithologist and I would often visit Jesmond Dene to spend hours on end watching the beautiful mute swans as they paddled up and down the river in search of food to feed their young. It's so sad to think that they are gone now, and I hope that one day they will return to breed here.

The Ouseburn Board School, now a business development centre ran by the council. One of the towers is said to be haunted.

What follows is an extract taken from Mike's book, reproduced verbatim. It is a wonderful account and it is a tribute to the lost birds of Jesmond Dene:

> Not long after Lord Armstrong bequeathed the park to the people of Newcastle upon Tyne in the 1880s, swans began to nest on the Dene itself. These proved to be a particular attraction to visitors and gained an almost royal status. But by 1990 they were no longer to be found on the Dene. According to some, they were either killed or driven off by mindless hooligans, and, sadly, they're probably right. Now, it seems, the only swans to grace the skies over Jesmond Dene may be of the spectral kind.
>
> Tourist Tony Smith said he'd 'read about them in a book years ago' although he couldn't remember which one. 'I've heard about them, yes ... but I've never seen them. They're supposed to be the spirits of the dead or something. My aunt lives in Kenton, and she said she knew someone who claimed to have seen them, but I don't know; maybe she just read the same book as me and her imagination got the better of her!
>
> Ethel – who didn't want her surname or address immortalised in print – said that she may indeed have seen the Ghost Birds but wasn't sure. She claimed that in 2002, when she was a sprightly sixty-seven-year-old, she'd brought her great-grandson to the park for a walk. She could not recall exactly when, but believed that it was 'during the school holidays', which means the incident likely took place in the month of August. 'We were walking along the river, when we suddenly heard a fluttering noise in the trees to our left. I turned and looked, but couldn't see anything. Mark said, "What was that, Grandma?" I honestly didn't know what it was, so we walked on. A minute or two later we heard it again, but this time I looked up and for a brief second I saw some things fluttering above my head. I couldn't make out what they were, because for some reason I couldn't seem to make out their shape, but they were something like big birds. It was all very strange, and I started to feel a bit uncomfortable. Mark and I quickly walked back up the path the way we had come. Later I mentioned what I'd seen to my husband, and he said that they had probably been bats. The thing was I've seen bats before, and these didn't seem like bats to me. I told my husband that bats only came out like that at night, but he insisted that it was probably bats I'd seen. I still don't think so.'
>
> The insubstantial nature of the 'things' seen by Ethel is intriguing, but if the witnessing of the Ghost Birds is fascinating in itself, working out exactly what type of phenomenon they may be is even more so. Superficially, one could argue that, if they exist, the spectral birds are as their epithet suggests; ghosts. Animal ghosts are not as common as their human equivalents, but they certainly aren't unknown.

three

NEWCASTLE'S HAUNTED PUBS AND INNS

The Bird's Nest Pub – Walker – (Now demolished)

The Bird's Nest public house was located at the far west end of Walker Road in St Anthony's estate which is in the east end of the city. Just along the old back lane stood its sister drinking establishment, The Bird's Nest Club, and both these buildings are now long gone, demolished in the 1980s. The club was accidentally burned down one day and following this it was decided that the pub (along with the houses in the back lane) would also be brought down as plans were in the pipeline for a new development scheme.

The Bird's Nest bar was not that large, and consisted of two floors; the upper floor being the living area for the pub landlord and family, and the lower floor the actual pub and lounge. It was a plain, whitewashed building that served as a drinking den for the 'Walker locals'. During my childhood I spent most of my time 'knockin aboot' in the area of the pub and its neighbourhood, as this was where I was born and raised. For a brief period of time I became friendly with a girl called Linda who was the daughter of the (then) landlord of the pub. As a friend of Linda, I was allowed into the pub's living apartment to play on rainy days and it was only on these occasions I managed to get into the premises.

I vaguely remember Linda telling me that she thought the pub was haunted. She told me about the occasions when she had heard the sounds of footsteps moving across the floor when she knew everyone else was asleep in the household, with the pub being closed up and the bar being empty. The noises, she concluded, could not have come from downstairs. This frightened her to some extent. Along with the strange footsteps being heard, she also mentioned that, on other occasions, the bottles and glasses could be heard 'clinking' and 'tinkling' in the vicinity below her living quarters – in the bar.

Gone, but not forgotten; the Bird's Nest pub in Walker.

She likened it to the sound of the glass collector being busy at work – although, once again, the pub was closed up and empty.

Interesting anecdotes to say the least, but we must take into account the fact that I was quite young at the time, as was Linda, and friends at that age can … well, misinterpret these things and then perhaps exaggerate or embellish them! Kids do love to tell 'spooky stories' to their friends, so it won't be too hard to perhaps give rational explanations for these accounts; having said that, you just don't know. So, were these events kids' stories or real paranormal happenings? I can't say for sure, but one thing I did notice – the family didn't reside at the Bird's Nest pub for very long …

The Carriage – Jesmond Railway Station

Jesmond railway station is a Grade II listed building that was constructed around 1864 and was subsequently converted into a charming and atmospheric public house in the early 1980s. It is now known as The Carriage, although the actual railway carriage itself (housed outside on the tracks) is in fact a restaurant. The pub has retained some of the original features from its time as a railway station, which of course adds to an already delightful and ambient eating and drinking atmosphere.

It appears the old station is not just home to its owners but also an ethereal visitor from the otherworld pops in from time to time and makes his presence known. The phantom often does this by standing close behind people – a little too close, some say – and many reports of this occurring have come in over the years. One individual actually moved to one side to let 'whoever it was behind them' get past; of course, no one was there actually there.

Known as George, this phantom was said (at one time, but not so much these days) to make himself known almost on a daily basis at the pub, and visitors and staff alike had embraced and accepted him just as though he was one of the regulars. However, George the friendly phantom is not the only ghost said to reside there.

The ghost of an unknown lady is also said to stalk the building creating poltergeist-like activity. Things have been thrown around on the premises, doors have been known to slam closed when no one is around, glasses are broken and objects have been moved from their original positions (only to be later found stacked up in geometrical structures).

I called in a year or two ago to find out if anything had been going on there recently, only to be told, 'the place has no ghosts and nothing odd has been experienced here'. I wondered if perhaps the chap I spoke to was new to the pub. He didn't seem to be a local person judging by his accent, so perhaps he was unaware of the pub's spooky reputation.

An interesting postscript follows my visit. One night not too long ago I was giving a talk at a presentation about the paranormal; the venue was Castle Bolton in North Yorkshire. After my talk I was approached by a woman who asked where I lived. She then told me she was from the Jesmond area of the city and took it upon herself to tell me all about her paranormal experiences. She relayed a number of experiences to me (as many folk do), but one particular account was of considerable interest. She was sitting in a local pub waiting for a friend, and had decided to read while she waited. As she was sitting in the corner, with her head buried in her newspaper, she heard someone approach her; she then heard 'something move' on the seat next to her. Shuffling noises followed, as though someone was sitting down in the seat concerned.

Engrossed in her newspaper, she assumed the commotion was her friend arriving for lunch. She hurriedly read the last few lines of her article and then lowered the paper to greet her friend – but to her utter surprise, no one was there and the bar was still completely empty, apart from a barman leaning on the far counter. Five minutes later her friend ambled into the pub and they had their lunch. I asked the lady where this incident took place and was subsequently told, 'Oh it was a lovely bar near the university, can't remember its name now ... The Railway? No, I think it's called The Carriage!'

The Old George

The Old George is a fine drinking den that is nicely tucked away down an ancient, cobbled back lane called 'Old George Yard' and is situated to the east of Newcastle's Cloth Market. The pub is believed to be one of the oldest pubs in Newcastle upon Tyne and has been described as an out-and-out oasis of tranquillity in an otherwise disturbed world. Looking at the pub from the cobble-stoned lane outside, one gets the impression of a traditional-style olde-worlde pub serving fine ales and beers – and you would be right, for this is exactly what the Old George is. It actually dates back to the early 1600s, and was once used as a coaching inn. It is also believed that there are royal connections to the pub. King Charles I reputedly drank there back in the seventeenth century.

The Old George in Central Newcastle, the one-time drinking den of King Charles I. His ghost is said to be seen here on occasions.

A replica (I am told) of the chair that Charles I used during his visits to the Old George.

There is a room at the inn named after him, and a chair he allegedly once sat in to 'sup his ale' is still there. However, I was informed that the chair is actually a reproduction of the original.

Stepping inside the Old George Inn, as I have done quite often – in the name of research, of course – is figuratively taking a step back in time. The past comes to life and one is automatically taken into the world of yesteryear: a large, open fire sits near the main entrance, the walls are panelled and the Old George retains its ancient, low ceilings with thick, oak beams. These give the inn an air of grandeur and magnificence that is still obvious to the visitor – even after 400 years or so.

Like all ancient hostelries, it too has its resident ghost; as a matter of fact, the Old George is known as one of the North East's most famous 'haunted pubs'. Perhaps it is famous because the ghost that is said to reside there is none other than King Charles I himself. Along with phantom footfalls across the wooden floors in the empty rooms, the spectre of King Charles I has reputedly been seen standing at the bar – complete with his head!

The Black Boy Inn

The Black Boy Inn, or 'Blackie Boy', as it is more commonly known, is located in Newcastle city centre on the famous 'Groat Market', which stands opposite the Bigg Market, and is one of the city's better-known haunted pubs. It is only a stone's throw away from The Old George Inn, and, like the Old George, it backs onto an old cobblestone yard. Established in 1823, the Black Boy Inn currently serves food as well as the traditional alcoholic beverages. This pub was once the favourite drinking den of North-East born engraver and naturalist, Thomas Bewick.

The Blackie Boy has three levels, with a long bar on the ground floor – complete with an old library – and a clock behind the bar dating back to 1923. Upstairs there is a function room that is used for parties. The third or top level is currently used for storage. The ghost, it is said, resides on the second floor.

There are a few theories regarding whom or what the ghost of the Blackie Boy really is, and why it should haunt there; in all honesty I think that no one knows the real truth behind the legend. During my research I spoke with the sub-manager, Steven Hickman. He informed me that he always knew the pub had a 'haunted reputation' and he'd heard strange stories from bar staff past and present.

Staff members have admitted to seeing dark shadows flitting about and an eerie presence has been detected by a few. Of course this could be nothing more than auto-suggestion on the part of nervous and weary pub workers who are well aware of the bar's reputation.

Steven also told me a few stories of ghostly phenomena that are a little harder to explain, including a chilling account from one former employee. While working on the second floor, this particular individual heard what could only be described as a 'harrowing scream' followed by a malevolent voice commanding her to 'Get out, get out!' Auto-suggestion? I don't think so.

The Blackie Boy in the Groat Market is said to be very haunted and was a one-time favourite drinking den of North-East born engraver and naturalist, Thomas Bewick.

Thomas Bewick, a frequenter of haunted pubs.

Steven also admitted to me that he had a paranormal experience of his own once. One afternoon he was on his way to 'pay a visit' whilst working up on the second floor. As he strolled across the function room towards the loos he noticed that the door leading into the gents was open. It then slammed shut in what seemed to be a controlled fashion. At first he wondered if a gust of wind, or a draught, could have been responsible. These explanations were ruled out when, on examination, the windows were found to be closed. Besides, the door was an old, heavy one of robust construction and it would have taken a gale-force wind to move it.

Feeling quite scared, he retreated downstairs to think about what he had just witnessed and decided to 'pay his visit' on the first floor instead. After pondering his encounter, he became convinced that it must have had a paranormal origin.

So there you have it: the second floor of the Blackie Boy continues to live up to its famous reputation, sometimes by scaring the staff witless!

Bob Trollop's

Bob Trollop's is an aged, traditional timber-framed Newcastle alehouse. It is located in the Sandhill area of the Quayside, and is part of the Wessex Taverns' chain of public houses – as are the neighbouring Red House and Offshore 44. This most welcoming inn has wooden beams on the ceiling and a sturdy wooden floor, giving the pub its ancient, olde-worlde feel.

Bob Trollop's.

The blocked-off stairwell in Bob Trollop's. This is where the sounds of footsteps (thought to belong to one-time landlady Margaret Reay) have been heard coming down the stairs.

A colleague of mine, Steve Taylor, who is the man behind Newcastle's very successful ghost walks, tells me that at one time Bob Trollop's pub was a house of ill-repute, and that it was owned by one Margaret Reay in 1840. It appears that the basement area of the pub was used as the 'knocking shop' for four women, and it is said that one of the girls had brought back a man for some salacious night-time fun when an argument broke out – over what, he couldn't say. It then got out of hand. The drunken man in question is believed to have picked up an oil lamp – used to light the cellars – and smashed it over the young prostitute, thus setting fire to her. This wicked act resulted in the burning to death of the young lady of the night.

Yet it is not the murder victim that is said to haunt Bob Trollop's, but the old owner, Margaret Reay. Steve went on to say, 'In the pub at the back there is a boarded-up stairwell of which the last few stairs can clearly be seen. They come down from the above floor and protrude into the bar area, and it is these stairs where the ghost of Margaret can be heard as she paces down them to enter the room'.

The manager, Joyce Wemyss, confirmed this when I visited the pub during my research. She had heard the footsteps on occasions, as have a number of the bar staff whom I spoke to while researching this book.

Other mysterious phenomena have been reported there too. The room above Bob Trollop's, where the blocked-off stairwell leads to the upper floor, is the function room that belongs to the Quilted Camel Club. It is in this room from which thumps and bangs have been heard to emanate when no one is upstairs.

The Red House – the scene of a ghost that has only ever been witnessed once.

The Tyne Bridge and Guild Hall as seen from the Red House.

'It's as though someone was stomping around up there with boots on', I was told. I had an interesting time down at Bob Trollop's, researching the ghosts and having a good look around. During my visit there, I was also able to visit and learn about another two wonderfully haunted inns – Offshore 44 and the Red House. They are right beside one another, and all three pubs are run by Joyce.

The Red House

The Red House stands next to Bob Trollop's on the Quayside, and from the front window one can enjoy splendid views of the Guild Hall and Tyne Bridge as it spans the river and joins Newcastle with Gateshead. It is probably one of Newcastle's oldest (and smallest) public houses and has amazing stone walls and floors. With a quaint little passage that takes the reveller to neighbouring drinking establishments, the Red House pub sells some of the finest guest ales one could ever wish to imbibe.

At the back of the pub there is a small but comfortable lounge that has only one way in and one way out. It is here where the 'ghost man' has been seen. On the one and only occasion the phantom was witnessed, he was observed walking into this lounge area. A courting couple, out for a drink, had placed their orders at the bar and had decided to follow the chap into the lounge area where they could happily get lost in each other's eyes while drinking away their 'hard earned' more or less undisturbed – but disturbed they were when they walked into the lounge to find no one else was in there. Where had the other man gone? Surely he couldn't have slipped back out unnoticed? It seems that, as they had literally followed him in after buying their drinks, there was no way he could have come back out without them realising. When they reported this strange occurrence to the staff they knew nothing of the mystery guest in the pub. They had not served nor even seen him anywhere in the pub. Those that frequent this pub will know that if someone walks past the bar – or even merely pops their head in the door – they are noticed, as the pub is really small.

The ghost – if it was a ghost – had never been seen before that day and has never (to the knowledge of the owners and staff) been seen again. One wonders on just what date it was seen and whether or not it may be some kind of anniversary haunting – I guess we will never know for certain.

Offshore 44

Offshore 44 is a splendid drinking den with a very high ceiling, a solid stone floor – and, like all good, old-fashioned pubs, wooden beams on the ceilings. The interior is marvellously festooned with nautical features such as ships' steering wheels, beer barrels, ropes, nets, buoys, and even large models of galleons and schooners. When

Offshore 44.

Bessie Surtees' House and Offshore 44 in Sandhill. (Courtesy of Walter Ritson)

you step inside, you are taken back to the days of smugglers, sailors and press gangs. However, don't be fooled by the theme of the pub, as that is all it is – a seafaring theme. Actually, before the building was used as a pub it was once a shop.

The back wall in the building is said to form the outer walls of the old Newcastle walls, and it is believed that this area was where the corpses of criminals were displayed after the malefactor in question had been hanged on the gallows. I must admit that looking at this wall, and comparing the area to old maps of Newcastle, this could well be the case.

During the compilation of this book I made many visits to alleged haunted pubs and inns. I sampled a good variety of ales along the way, listened to tales of yesteryear and relished the wonderful ghost accounts that many kinds of people, from all walks of life, relayed to me. This pub was no different. I was informed by one of the bar staff that when they were in the bar alone, tending to their duties, they were always looking over their shoulder and listening out for strange and unexplained noises. The barman believes that when he was alone … well, he actually wasn't alone, if you catch my drift. A sudden 'sense of presence' would envelope him from time to time, the eerie feeling that that someone, or 'something from the other side', may not have been too far away. When asked whether he liked working there side-by-side with a ghost, he simply replied, 'No, not on my own … but I just get on with it'.

The Cooperage Pub, one of the most famous haunted inns of Newcastle.

Another fascinating account came from my colleague Steve Taylor. He went on to tell me,'I witnessed what looked like a man in a blue, velvet jacket with ruffles around the neck but worn very loose. It was rather unnerving to see, and it made me feel rather unwell. Another odd thing I noticed was that he was displaced from the visible setting, as if he was sitting behind the seating'.

I was also informed about the 'resident psychics' who have often visited the premises – one of them being related to the manager. They too have sensed otherworldly individuals, with one tale concerning a man who had somehow had his arm ripped from its socket on the premises and subsequently bled to death. However, details of this alleged incident are rather difficult to obtain. With other stories of bloodletting, witchcraft, murders, public exhibitions of the recently executed, and black magic, it is no wonder that this pub lays claims to having a spectre or two.

The Cooperage

The Cooperage is located on Newcastle upon Tyne's historic Quayside and is by far the oldest pub in the city, dating back to the 1300s. This magnificent old building was a cooper's workshop in the nineteenth century, hence the current name of this charming old drinking house.

The beams on the exterior of the building gives the pub a Tudor look. Like many ancient taverns and inns, the Cooperage sells some of the best real ales available, making it a popular attraction for locals, Quayside revellers, and students. Of course, although this beautiful old pub holds its original charm, character, and ambience, some say it retains more than that. The building itself is soaked with local folklore and superstition, and I must admit that when I step inside I cannot help but feel the atmosphere change; not for the worse, I hasten to add, but there is a palpable change in the atmosphere nonetheless.

The Cooperage Long Stairs, said to be where a brutal murder once took place when the victim was nailed to the door.

Rumour has it that many, many years ago a visiting sailor whose ship was birthed at Newcastle Quayside was accosted by some locals (or according to some, other visiting sailors – no one knows for sure). For whatever reason, they assaulted the sailor in a most horrific manner: the man was nailed to the side door of the pub that leads out onto the old stone flight of steps called Long Stairs that run up past the Cooperage itself. It is alleged that the original door still occupies the current door aperture, and it is said you can still see the original nail holes. I ventured down to the Cooperage for a peek one day, but, alas, could find no trace of the aforementioned nail holes in the door, which is now not in use and may not be the original fixture anyway.

Needless to say, this unfortunate chap died due to his injuries, and it is said his ghost has been seen both inside the pub and outside on the stone stairwell where he was so brutally murdered.

Another, better-known spectre was seen in the 1970s on the upper floor of the inn, in what now serves as the function room. Apparently, the cleaner reported for work one morning and was eager to get on with her duties. The bar had been busy the night before as there has been a function on, so where better to start than at the top in the function room and work her way down? She meandered into the function room, cloth in hand, and began to pick up the empty bottles whilst cleaning the tables and emptying the ashtrays. During her work she became aware that someone was in the room with her, so she looked up across the room and saw a 'white, misty cloud' floating over by one of the tables. Shaking with fear, she remained fixed to the spot watching this misty apparition until it began to move across the floor towards her, all the while becoming larger and more human-shaped. Not surprisingly, she dropped her cleaning gear and ran like never before down the stairs and out the building. She never returned.

This is by far the most famous ghost story attached to the Cooperage, but there are persistent rumours that poltergeist-like activity occurs in the bars on the ground floor. Lights switch themselves on and off, glasses are sometimes thrown around and witnesses often mention feeling a 'sense of presence'. Who knows, perhaps it is the unfortunate sailor who was nailed to the door?

Regardless of what or who the ghosts are or why they remain here, I can safely say that the Cooperage pub has to be one of the finest haunted establishments I have visited during my research. I must also pay tribute to the friendly landlord whose hospitality I enjoyed whilst supping a pint of his finest.

The Bridge Hotel

The Bridge Hotel stands next to the Castle Garth and commands a spectacular view across the River Tyne and Newcastle Quayside from the beer garden at the back, which is situated precisely in the middle of the ruined and gaunt Newcastle city walls. The land the pub is built upon was once was a medieval site and housed both a Saxon burial ground and a Roman fortress. Stories persist of a tunnel leading from the pub cellars under the now cobbled car park and into the neighbouring Castle Keep, but I

The Bridge Hotel taken from the roof of Newcastle Keep. A fine drinking house which was reputed to have experienced strange, ghostly happenings.

can't find any evidence to corroborate this. Both stewards at the pub and at Newcastle Keep know nothing about this, and suggest that it would not be plausible for the area between the two buildings to contain such a tunnel. However, Castle Keep curator Paul McDonald told me that the pub in question over the road 'had been investigated' by a local research team after hearing that mysterious 'dark figures had been seen and later reported in the ladies' loos' (situated downstairs near the cellars). When the witnesses checked to see if anyone was there at the time, they found they were on their own.

The function rooms upstairs are also reputed to be haunted (if the psychics from the society that once met here are to be believed) by a dark figure of a man that has been both sensed and seen standing behind the counter in the bar.

Regardless of whether the pub is haunted or not, the land it is built upon most certainly is. A well-known and respected television medium, and correspondent of mine, once visited the site and subsequently saw the ghost of a Roman soldier standing outside the castle at the precise area where the main settlement once stood. The full story can be read in part two.

Four

INVESTIGATIONS AND OVERNIGHT CASE STUDIES

Byker Community Centre – Newcastle East

Byker Community Centre is a large three-storey building situated in the east end of Newcastle and was built in 1928. Unlike modern-day community centres, inside the building there is a ground-floor basement and an apartment flat where the caretaker once would have lived. It has a spacious hall, along with kitchens, an office on the ground floor and a huge, old ballroom and stage on the second floor.

Over the years the building has had an array of different uses, including a church hall (it once belonged to the local church which stands adjacent to the community centre, and to this day stands on what is hallowed ground). The Boys' Brigade and Girl Guides frequented the building in years gone by, and as far back as records show the building has been a ballroom and dancehall for the more mature members of the community.

In more recent times, activities such as badminton, table tennis and martial arts have often been practised in the building and scenes from the children's television series *Byker Grove* were often filmed in the large hall there. Since the early 1990s there has been a judo club there, at which the author, a black belt, was a judo instructor.

In the early days, before the centre was built, the land was the original Byker Farm and estate; in the 1920s the farm was demolished to make way for the community building. This magnificent building survived the bombing raids of the Second World War and was used as a refuge and hospital for the local victims of the bombing who lost their homes and were seriously injured during 1939-1945. It goes without saying that some of these unfortunate victims of the German bombings would have died of horrific injuries inside this building. It is not hard to imagine the pain suffered by these

Byker Community Centre in the morning mist.

individuals; the hurt, the anguish and the torment of knowing nothing could be done to save them, all this may still somehow be recorded in the fabric of the building.

In my role as judo instructor, I was often in the building and I spent quite a bit of time chatting to the community workers who organise events and look after the place. They would often tell me stories about strange goings-on and how they thought that ghosts inhabited the centre. I was told that on a number of occasions when the staff members were downstairs they often felt they were not alone and were being watched. When they turned around, no one was there. Footsteps have also been heard in empty rooms, but one of the more eerie events was when the cleaner opened up the building and heard the piano on the top floor playing. Upon a brave inspection, the music stopped. She was the only person in the centre.

A more sinister ghost has been said to glide from one room to another on the ground floor and takes the form of a tall, black shadow. The former caretaker and odd-job man told me he has seen this spectre on a number of occasions. So we have a large, old building with a ghost on each floor. I also experienced the odd happening while in the centre on my own and, although I took great interest, I was not actually investigating the paranormal at that point in my life. However, in May 2003 I started my investigations and what better place to begin than the community centre at Byker? I knew the people there and I was a member.

An eerie-looking view of the building from the neighbouring churchyard.

I got permission to spend the night there and thus began a series of paranormal investigations into the alleged haunting of the centre. The first overnight investigation proved quite interesting, to say the least! I recorded some sudden drops in temperature and I actually heard the shuffling of feet coming from the basement hall. Upon investigation I found the room was empty. This, I thought, was a good time to leave my tape recorder on in the hope that I might pick up or record some paranormal activity. I was not disappointed, because when I listened to the recording after the investigation I heard what I believed – and still believe – to be three or four distinct footfalls across the wooden floor. I had captured phantom footsteps. All this – combined with the interior doors at the entrance to the building violently rattling and shaking at about 3 a.m. – proved my efforts were certainly not in vain.

Our team carried out a second investigation about one year later which proved to be even more exciting. We had the usual array of monitored activity (such as temperature drops and photographic evidence of light anomalies), but the most interesting and frightening happening was when I was physically touched on the arm in one of the storerooms adjacent to the basement hall. I nearly fell over trying to flee the room in terror, as I knew that no member of the team was near me.

We left this room for a while and upon our return we could all feel a sense of foreboding coming from that room. It was also noted that when you approached the

The stairwell in Byker Community Centre where mysterious footsteps have been heard.

doorway to the room, the air was ice cold. It was like walking into a freezer, yet five minutes earlier the room was a nice, ambient temperature. It was so cold you could actually see your breath. There was something otherworldly in that room, but who – or what – was it? We had a very sceptical and scientific-minded investigator with us that night, but he was not sceptical for long! After an incident earlier on involving a door that slammed shut twice after we had secured it in an open position, he was convinced something strange was indeed going on. This investigation proved too much for us and we closed it down at 3 a.m. and left the building.

We went back a month or two later to continue our investigations. The team arrived at 9.30 p.m., and by 11 p.m. we had begun. What impressed me most about this investigation was that the psychics I had asked along as guests picked up on events and happenings I know for a fact they could not have previously heard of. At the time this building could not be researched on the internet, and none of them visited the place prior to this investigation. All my results and findings from the previous investigations were kept under lock and key and no one was aware of those results; neither did they know the ghost stories attached to the building.

Some amazing suggestions were produced by the psychics, including our team psychic, Suzanne, who picked up on the fact that footsteps had been heard in the basement and the door upstairs was known to have slammed shut. Previous investigations proved this to be the case. Suzanne also picked up on the ghost of a dark figure, and told me exactly where he had been seen moving around on the ground floor. This was in the same spot where the former caretaker had seen the tall, black shadow glide from room to room. Glenn Hall, our other team psychic, also picked up the fact that the centre had once been used as a hospital or somewhere to tend to the wounded. He said he could sense surgical spirits and got the impressions of injuries and pain.

This is also correct; I remind the reader of the bombing during the Second World War that I mentioned earlier, and the injuries sustained by the very people taking refuge in the centre. One more piece of very impressive psychic ability was produced by one of the guest psychics. She told me while walking around the building that one or two people had passed on quite recently into the spirit world whilst in that very location. She told me where and how she thought these people had died. It turned out she was correct with her impressions.

During this investigation, while in the large hall on the second floor, a guest investigator and psychic sat down next to where I know someone had passed on and claimed to see and feel someone sitting on the seat next to her. She got a fright when she realised it was not any of the team investigators. However, for obvious reasons, and due to our code of ethics, I cannot name these people or state how they died. Needless to say, these residual energies are still lingering in the community centre and are there to be picked up on at certain times. It must be stressed that these energies are just that: energy. These recently departed souls who passed into the spirit world are very likely resting in peace, and the energy that is left over from years of visiting this centre is what is recorded in the building. This is what is left for the psychics to pick up on.

However, I do feel that there are some active spirits and ghosts that inhabit this old building who are quite mischievous to say the least. This conclusion has been reached due to the fact that lots of strange, inexplicable occurrences have happened and have been recorded by the North East Ghost Research Team. There are also the tales and stories that were relayed to me by mature, credible and responsible witnesses. Although the building has not been around for a long time, it's been around long enough to store, record and house residual energies and active spirits, which will still be there in years to come.

The Fusilier Pub – Forrest Hall

The Fusilier public house is a huge building situated in the Forrest Hall area of Newcastle upon Tyne. The Fusilier is a pub with a difference: it has an air of grandeur, much like an old stately home. The grand staircase leading to the upper function rooms has a graceful wooden balustrade, a beautiful, soft-carpeted stairwell and oak-panelled walls. It is a staircase that could equal those found in most palaces, castles and stately homes of noble splendour.

Contrary to what people may think, and how the building looks, it is not an old pub and was built less than seventy-five years ago. It is of splendid construction inside and

The Fusilier public house.

out, and it is easy to assume that the Fusilier is much older that it actually is. Having said that, in seventy-five years the building may still be able to store and house psychic, residual echoes and energies from its short but eventful past, and it seems that this is what has happened.

During an interview conducted prior to our investigation we were informed by the (then) landlord and landlady, Lee and Kelly, that ghostly occurrences happen at the pub on a regular basis. Footsteps have often been heard emanating from an area where nobody was actually present. Glasses and bottles have been heard moving and clinking while the bar areas were completely empty. A former male employee of the pub from a few years back, called Harry, is said to haunt the snug area, and the ghost of a young girl aged between five and eight years old is said to haunt the beautiful old stairwell. A trusted member of the North East Ghost Research Team conducted the interview and all details ascertained on this 'pre-investigation chat' were, as always, kept from the team psychics.

On the night of the investigation members of the North East Ghost Research Team joined Team Phenomena (now disbanded) for an exploration of the pub. We arrived at about 10 p.m., made our way to the 'snug' area and prepared for the investigation.

The North East Ghost Research Team psychic, Glenn Hall, was to conduct a 'reading' of the premises to see if he could pick up who haunts the pub, and where the ghostly 'hotspots' are located within this locale. Suzanne Hitchinson was on hand to take notes and orchestrate the psychic reading. The reading began on the upper level of the pub in the large function room. Glenn picked nothing up. However, on approaching the grand stairwell from the top, he seemed to sense 'spirit energy'.

The grand staircase where the ghost of a girl was sensed by psychic Glenn Hall.

He picked up on a female teenager and the letter 'M'. On walking to the bottom of the stairs he sensed another 'spirit energy', only this time it was that of a younger girl. He said she had been seen on the stairwell in the past by visitors, and was more startling than frightening. This statement from Glenn proved to be correct, as a young girl had indeed been seen on the stairwell previously.

As the investigators walked through the doors at the bottom of the stairs, which lead to the corridor, Glenn told us that he still felt the young girl with him. He went on to say that this area was once used as a main entrance to the building, although now there are no traces of any old doorways. The landlord and landlady also confirmed this as true.

The teams then proceeded to the downstairs function room and Glenn mentioned that he could smell cigar smoke. This was a psychic impression, and he told us that people had actually smelt the odour of these cigars in this area before while no one was actually smoking in the building. Again, this was confirmed by the owners, who went on to tell us that the cleaners and bar staff had indeed smelt smoke, sometimes before the pub had even opened. Described as a 'strong, pungent smell', the aroma could not have had a natural cause due to the fact that no one in the building was smoking at these times. Glenn went on to say that he could sense a 'spirit animal' that hung around in this area. He said it was a dog. The investigators were then told that a ghost dog had indeed been seen scampering around the function area. One witness, we were told, was said to have seen it disappear before his very eyes.

The researchers then ventured into the snug area of the pub to continue the reading. Glenn sensed the spirit of a man, with whom he sensed a 'foreign connection'.

An artist's impression of a phantom woman as she descends the grand staircase. (Illustration by Julie Olley)

Now there is said to be the ghost of a man that haunts that room, the aforementioned Harry. Harry, by all accounts, was the son of the former pub owners when the inn first opened, and he worked there, cleaning the ashtrays and collecting glasses. The team members were informed that Harry was a 'disabled person with a curvature of the spine'. He was also, they were told, a very bad-tempered and hot-headed person. No one is sure how Harry met his end, but the investigators were informed that it was there at that very pub where he died. The snug area, now called 'Harry's Snug', is where his body lay for seven days before the funeral. The reading ended downstairs in the subterranean vaults where a gaunt-looking male, about 5ft 10in tall, who allegedly 'needed some attention', was said to reside. Who he was or why he haunts this place no one knows. It is interesting to add that although Glenn seemingly sensed the spirit of the man down there, no first-hand accounts of his activities have been otherwise reported.

At 1 a.m. the night vigils began with my group investigating the stairwell and corridor. I informed Suzanne, who was taking notes, that I had the impression a suicide had taken place in that area, more specifically, a hanging. I 'called out to the atmosphere' in the hope of enticing some spiritual activity, but to no avail. We then sat in silence for a while and just observed. Again, Glenn sensed 'energy' and it seemed to be moving around at the top of the stairwell, but an electro-magnetic field (EMF) reading in this area proved negative. However, a 4-degree temperature drop was recorded, indicating that something odd may indeed have been occurring at the top of the stairs. Draughts from open doors and windows, and other possible natural causes, were eliminated upon further investigation. Glenn then astounded me by saying he felt as though a hanging had taken place on this stairwell – my impression had already been written down in Suzanne's notes. However, subsequent research has shown that no hanging or suicide (at least on record) had taken place there. Others in this same area felt that invisible hands had touched them and one investigator said she felt two hands pushing upon her back when no one was behind her.

I then mentioned that I got the impression of a 'ghost lady' that may have walked the stairs there. Again, this tied in with what Glenn had also sensed earlier on. Glenn then told the investigators that the female ghost seen on the stairs wore a long, flowing dress and that she dated back to the 1960s – and again, the pub owners confirmed this, and indeed had seen her themselves.

Glenn then complained that he was feeling a tightness or restriction in his chest and at this point had to take a rest. A final odd occurrence happened during this vigil: three of the investigators present claimed to have seen with their own eyes a phosphorescent glow floating around the bottom of the stairwell. When I took a photograph of that area there was indeed a strange glow emanating from one area of the photograph – coincidence, or spiritual activity?

The second location for investigation was the main bar area. The room temperature read 20 degrees and no EMF anomalies were recorded. The shuffling of footsteps was then heard by an investigator, followed by the sound of the seats moving and banging together. At this point in the investigation I set up some trigger objects on the bar and began recording them with my video camera. I was casually chatting to Glenn Hall at the bar when we were distracted simultaneously by the same thing: through the other side of the bar, in Harry's Snug, we could both clearly see an anthropomorphic black shadow moving around the room at considerable speed. It was as though a video recording of someone moving around had been speeded up. On the night I described it as being 'like something from *The X Files*' as it was so strange. It was real, it shook both of us up and it is something we are at a total loss to explain. Glenn then sensed that a male person in the bar area, who had recently made his presence known to him, did not want 'snooping investigators'. Glenn then told the researchers that this male figure was 'grouchy!' Could it have been the spirit of Harry?

The third location was down in the cellars, and although much information was forthcoming from the team psychic, interviews with the staff, pub owners and subsequent research did not verify anything. However, upon checking the dictation machine after the investigation, three loud bangs could be heard on the cassette which we had not heard at the time of recording. After the cellar vigil the investigators all decided to sit in Harry's Snug in total silence to merely observe, listen, and wait for anything paranormal to occur. It did not.

Newcastle Keep and Black Gate.

And so the investigation at the Fusilier pub came to an end. It had proved to be an eventful evening with some extraordinary phenomena occurring. Whether or not it was down to the ghosts of the Fusilier we cannot say for sure – yet! But one thing is certain, and that is that odd things do indeed happen at this pub. Two people witnessed the fast-moving anthropomorphic figure, one being myself. This is something I really couldn't stop thinking about for some time. I went over and over it in my mind, and it was one of the most spine-chilling things I have ever seen. Everything else that I witnessed on the night of our investigation pales in comparison. We packed up our equipment, said our goodbyes to Lee and Kelly, and told them we would be back to try and answer some of the questions thrown up on this amazing investigation.

Newcastle Keep – City Centre

It is believed the first fortification built on the site of the Newcastle Garth belonged to the Roman Empire in AD 120. In those days the fortress was called Pons Aelius and it was essentially built to safeguard and defend the bridge, called Pons Aelii, which was also built by the Romans and stood roughly where the Swing Bridge now stands.

It is believed that some time later an ancient Anglo-Saxon burial ground occupied the site, and modern-day archaeology has proved this to be so. Around 1,000 years later

The Elsdon Gibbet Post near Otterburn in Northumberland where William Winter was left hanging in his gibbet cage after he murdered Margaret Crozier in 1791.

the eldest son of William the Conqueror, Robert Curthose, built another fortress in 1080 on the same site with wood and earth. In the 1100s, during the reign of Henry II, it was constructed again from sandstone. The stone castle took five years (1172-1177) to build, at around a cost of £1,000-£1,500. This is what we see today, and it is a fine illustration of late Norman workmanship.

The castle's primary objective was the protection and defence of Newcastle, and as the site upon which it was built is on high ground, overlooking and dominating the valley, it was inevitable that the fort would be built in this spot. Nowadays its dominating position has been hidden by the modern edifices which have been developed around it.

After almost 1,000 years of sieges, invasions and bloody warfare, the castle was used as a common gaol, and for 200 years rapists, murderers, thieves and all kinds of petty criminals were held there under the most disgusting, cramped and squalid conditions. As you can imagine, sanitation was poor and disease was rife for the overcrowded inmates, and many deaths occurred due to these conditions.

One of the castle's more famous inmates was William Winter. He was allegedly held here after his trial at the Moot Hall before he was hanged in 1792 at Westgate in Newcastle. Winter murdered an old lady called Margaret Crozier in August 1791 in a place called Elsdon, which is about twenty miles east of Otterburn in Northumberland. His lifeless body was then taken to the scene of his crime where it was hung up in a gibbet cage as a deterrent to other would-be criminals. It is said that he haunts this lonely, barren and cold moor, longingly looking on from the roadside and staring at his gibbet post. Could William Winter also haunt the bowels of the Keep where once he was held as a prisoner? The gibbet post still stands to this day up on the moors at Elsdon and is known as 'Winter's Gibbet' or 'The Elsdon Gibbet'. A wooden head hangs from it. It is a chilling sight that would unnerve the most sceptical of people should they stumble across it one foggy evening.

Nowadays the Newcastle Keep is a popular museum and is owned by the Society of Antiquaries, as is the Black Gate that stands opposite. It is also the oldest and most historic building in Newcastle, so you can understand why this particular building was a must to investigate. During the past few years or so, I have taken part in no less than fifteen investigations with other research teams and ghost hunters from the region, and have encountered what I believe to be objective paranormal phenomena. On one occasion I saw a black shadow pass by the window and block out the light at the top of the stairs in the mezzanine chamber. This was accompanied by the shuffling of footsteps and, upon inspection, we found no one else in the vicinity. Others also witnessed this occurrence. On another occasion I heard a long drawn-out sigh coming from the empty Garrison Room and heard a disembodied muttering in my left ear while standing alone in the Queen's Chamber. This muttering was accompanied by breath on my ear and neck.

The account you are about to read is taken from two of the many investigations conducted by the North East Ghost Research Team. The two investigations were held within six months or so of each other. Our first visit to the castle was on 30 October (running in to the 31 October 2004), and one question was on my mind: 'Would Halloween make a difference to our investigation?' Well, we would find out soon enough, because as All Hallows' Eve began we held a séance in the Great Hall.

As midnight struck and the bells from Newcastle Cathedral rang out, we were all in a circle holding hands and attempting to communicate with the spirits of the Keep. During these proceedings it was reported that one investigator felt a constant, warm breath on the back of his neck although no one was actually behind him. It was also reported that two other investigators had felt chains around their necks tugged upon by unseen hands. More interestingly, one investigator claimed to have seen a bright, white mist in human form passing the doorway to the Great Hall as if it were heading up the stairwell to the galleries. So, all in all, an intriguing start to the investigation. It was after this séance we split into our groups to cover more of the castle.

During the course of the investigation various temperature drops were recorded, along with cold spots. At one point I actually felt something touch the side of my face (although no one was near me at the time). Also, EMF anomalies were recorded in abundance along with photographic evidence of light anomalies.

Another séance was held at 5 a.m., only this time in the Garrison Room and former prison. The séance lasted for forty-five or fifty minutes, and there were five sitters and one observer. This séance was quite productive and reports were coming in that sitters were being touched and prodded whilst, simultaneously, the room temperature dropped dramatically. The most interesting part of the proceedings was actually hearing footsteps and the shuffling of feet coming from outside the chapel area. We could all clearly hear these footfalls from inside the Garrison Room and when an investigator went to take a look, no one was there. Not a bad night's work; maybe running the investigation into Halloween was not such a bad idea after all ...

Our second investigation took place on 9 April 2005. It was a warm, clear night, and as usual we split into our teams and headed off into the castle. It was not long before the strange occurrences began. One of our guest investigators for the night, while in the Well Room, photographed an anomalous mist as the temperature dropped from 20 degrees to 14 degrees.

An exciting start! I called out to the atmosphere and asked if the spirits present would acknowledge us in any way, and at that precise time another photograph showing anomalous mist was taken.

At 12.30 p.m. a séance was held in the galleries in the upper section of the castle overlooking the Great Hall. It was reported earlier that two researchers in the vicinity saw a woman in an old, white dress. (This is not the first time investigators have reported the presence of a woman up there, as other ghost-hunting teams from the region have documented this phenomenon, as I found out after our investigation.) Our séance unfortunately proved rather fruitless, and nothing of any good evidential value was recorded or documented.

By 1 a.m. we were in the Garrison Room. A musty smell hit us all in the face; what it was, we do not know. After a few minutes in there, another investigator and I both clearly heard a long, drawn-out breath or sigh emanating from a part of the room in which no one was standing. This is a regular occurrence in the old prison. Could these sighs be the echoes from the past of the former prisoners and criminals who were once held in this very room awaiting certain death? It's a tantalising thought.

We ventured through to the chapel and this time we were greeted by a nice, sweet smell of what can only be described as incense. This was the only documented oddity during our vigil at this location. The hours passed, and all seemed to be quiet – until we held another séance downstairs in the Garrison Room. It was led by the North East Ghost Research Team's psychic, Suzanne Hitchinson (*née* McKay). We all stood in a big circle around the pillar in the centre of the room and held hands. I asked Suzanne to ask if the spirit of William Winter was with us.

A few positive responses were documented. Three video cameras, two of which were set up on tri-pods, turned themselves off completely whilst no one was near them. A black figure was seen inside the circle moving around. I know this to be true because it was I who saw it. It was at this point that Suzanne came over and stood behind me, which meant that we were both party to witnessing some of the most frightening phenomena of the night. As the séance was commencing I looked up to my right to see a black mass of dark energy (it's the only way I can describe it) in the corner. It came towards me over the tops of the heads of the other circle members. It came at some speed and, as it approached, I broke the circle and ducked to avoid it. By the time I had composed myself it had gone.

Had I stopped this thing in its tracks when I broke the circle and thus dispersed the energy it had somehow created? I cannot help thinking this was the case. I would have thought I was going mad had it not been for Suzanne's confirmation: she too saw the black mass from where she was standing directly behind me. During the pandemonium, three loud knocks were heard on the closed Garrison Room door and we all thought it was the castle warden coming down to see what all the noise was. It was not. When we opened the door, no one was there. The séance and the investigation ended at 4.30 a.m. and it had to have been one of the most remarkable investigations I'd run to that date. The old Keep at Newcastle is without question a hive of paranormal activity, and, in my opinion, the Garrison Room has to be the most haunted location in there. It is worth adding that a photograph of an alleged ghost has also been snapped here at Newcastle Keep. The photograph was taken by a colleague of mine back in March 2003 while investigating the castle with his research team. Here, in his own words, is Trevor Brown's account of how the image was captured:

> At 3 a.m. on Saturday 1 March 2003 I was in the King's Chamber talking with some individuals who were investigating that room when, suddenly, the Event Marshall came in and bellowed, 'Come and see this!' I thought she was just messing around, but nevertheless I went to take a look and luckily I had my camera ready. When I turned and faced the doorway from inside the King's Chamber I saw it! Across the hall and standing on top of the stairs leading up to another room was a misty apparition. It was a large, human-like shape that came down the stairs and then across the hall towards me. It looked as though it was reaching out with its left arm. I quickly raised my camera and clicked the shutter and took the photo. By this time all the hairs on my body were standing on end and my eyes started to stream with water. It was all over in a split second, but I managed to photograph it. The exact time of the photo was 3.11 a.m. Being sceptical in nature I had several sleepless nights trying to figure out just exactly what we had actually witnessed, but to no avail. I know it was not cigarette smoke as no one was allowed to smoke on our investigations. I try not to think about it anymore because it drives me insane wondering what the hell it was. I am grateful, however, for the experience and it is something I will never forget.

So, there you have it; Trevor's account of the Castle Keep spectre. Bringing things up to date, in the last few years I have visited the Keep on many more occasions, spent the night there and witnessed more odd goings-on.

One charity investigation I ran there in April 2006 was probably the biggest celebrity ghost hunt the North East has ever seen. Living TV's paranormal investigator Mark Webb was in attendance, along with Rachel Lacy – York's Ghostfinder General – and Diana Jarvis (a notable psychic investigator and former editor of *Vision* magazine) as well as other famous names in paranormal research. The event went really well and we raised more than £1,500 for the Children's Heart Unit fund. Unexplained footsteps were heard, temperature drops were detected and a fascinating photograph was taken by Mark Winter during this overnight study that caused considerable debate for months after the investigation.

So just remember, the next time you are visiting this wonderful museum and you suddenly feel anxious or unnerved for some reason, or perhaps it becomes a great deal colder, beware – you may not be on your own.

A photograph of an alleged ghost that was taken by Trevor Brown in Newcastle Keep. The apparition was seen by a number of people before the picture was taken. (Courtesy of Trevor Brown)

An anomalous mist in the King's Chamber, taken by the author during one of his many investigations at Newcastle Keep.

The Coroner's Court building on Newcastle Quayside where some strange activity was recorded by the Ghost and Hauntings Overnight Surveillance Team (G.H.O.S.T.).

The Coroner's Court – Newcastle Quayside

On the night of 24 February 2006, G.H.O.S.T. were due to investigate the Sea Nightclub on Newcastle Quayside, otherwise known as Neptune House. As the nightclub was open late we had to wait until 3 a.m. before we could get in to conduct our survey. Ironically, prior to this particular case study, we were allowed access into the Coroner's Court building, which stands adjacent to Sea. This venue had also never been investigated prior to the G.H.O.S.T. team's visit, and it is this investigation I will now elaborate upon.

This building was constructed in the late 1800s – around 1888 – and was once used as a mausoleum and morgue. It belongs to the same people as Sea and is more or less unused except for one room – and that is for administrative and managerial purposes. The team's event organiser, Lee Stephenson, was told by the property owners that they also felt this building was haunted. Strange occurrences and odd noises have been experienced by some of the staff while in there. An eerie 'sense of presence' had been felt and the sensation of being watched by invisible eyes has also been reported.

This section details the events that happened while the G.H.O.S.T. investigation team were in the court. On the night in question, we arrived at the premises at about 11.30 p.m. and immediately set about conducting our baseline tests and setting up our trigger objects. In the old morgue we set in place a wooden cross as a trigger object. The temperature read 13 degrees and no EMF anomalies were recorded. On the ground floor we placed another cross as a trigger object; the temperature read 4.5 degrees, and no EMF anomalies were recorded. On the upper floors no trigger object was used, but the room temperature was 3.5 degrees and again no EMF anomalies were detected. It should also be noted that as we were on the Quayside in Newcastle on a Friday night the chance of noise pollution was very high indeed. Great care was taken not to misinterpret any possible auditory phenomena.

We spilt into two groups to cover more of the building. Group one consisted of; Lee and Mark Winter (then a guest of the team) and I, while group two were; Drew Bartley, Fiona Vipond and Rob (guest and staff member). Our group stayed on the middle floor for the first vigil. At 12.55 a.m. I photographed my first light anomaly, so I called out into the atmosphere to see if anything would happen. We were not disappointed. A noise resembling a box falling or moving was heard by all present, although we were all sitting perfectly still at this point. I then tried to turn on my torch – I had just changed the batteries – but it would not work at all. We found this rather odd indeed.

We then ventured into the other room on the same level where we had placed motion sensors. As we were standing in the room the motion sensors were tripped and the alarm went off. It has to be stressed that the three investigators were nowhere near the sensors when they went off and further tests proved the batteries were working fine. They did not activate any more that night. A feeling of immense cold around the legs of Lee and Mark was reported just after the sensors were tripped, but this could have been a draught or cold breeze coming up the stairs from the cellars/old morgue. Lee and Mark hold differing views.

At this point, Lee caught some nice, moving light anomalies on video camera while the camera was facing the top of the stairs. We then ventured back into the other room to find our trigger object had been moved about an inch or so from its line. We took photographs of the moved cross and ended this first and very productive vigil.

It didn't take long for the team to work out that there was something very odd going on within the walls of this building. Group two was upstairs and they reported one or two strange noises and unexplained taps, but generally it was a quiet vigil for them.

Our next location saw us in the upper area of this building while the other group staked out the middle or ground floor. Within minutes of starting the vigil at 2 a.m., two moving light anomalies were caught on video camera. They both seemed to be caught around the loft hatch area on the ceiling. Lee stated that there might have been a hanging in this area, but subsequent research could not provide any validation for this suggestion.

I called out to the atmosphere, and once again Lee caught a strange light on the video camera. At this point in the investigation, I felt something actually touching the side of my face. It was like walking through cobwebs. I moved across the room and it happened again, only this time on the top of my head. I moved around again and once more it felt as though something was touching me. Very odd!

A trigger object used to entice spiritual activity.

The trigger object after it had been moved while in locked-off and controlled conditions.

Was something following me around the room? It certainly felt like it. Then, Lee's camera suddenly began to go in and out of focus (which happens quite a lot on investigations and is commonly reported by paranormal investigators all over). By now it was 2.30 a.m. and it was the end of the vigil. Team two came back from the downstairs morgue with some interesting results too: light anomalies were caught on night-vision video camera, and unexplained noises were heard coming from the stairwell. The phenomenon called 'pulsing' also occurred and was witnessed by everyone down there. This is when a certain part of the room goes darker and blacker than the rest of the room and then returns to normal. This happened in the doorway, and the light coming down the stairs was completely blacked out for some reason. Was this a trick of the light? Were the investigators' eyes playing tricks on them? Or was it paranormal phenomena? Whatever it is, it's pretty harrowing, as those who have been on paranormal investigations will testify. The group then ended their vigil with a séance in which Drew's left arm was grabbed and squeezed by what he described as an 'invisible presence'.

What would the rest of the night bring? It was our turn in the morgue, and I was very thrilled about the prospect of this vigil – little suspecting the terrifying events that were to follow. Vigil three started at 2.50 a.m. I began by calling out to the atmosphere. It was jet black down there, and you could not see your hand in front of your face.

At 2.55 a.m. we all heard a shuffling noise coming from the top of the stairs that led into the morgue. I ventured over to the bottom of the stairs, and the sounds became clearer. I called out to see if anyone was there and got no reply, so I climbed the stairs to investigate. Lo and behold, no one was there at all. So what was moving around on the stairs where, earlier on, our motion sensors were tripped? I could find no explanation, so I rejoined the group in the morgue, reported my findings and proceeded to call out to the atmosphere.

What Lee, Mark and myself then heard astounded us and sent shivers down our spines. We all heard a long, drawn-out breath that sounded almost like a guttural laugh. This was recorded on videotape. I continued to call out and, like the earlier group, we also experienced the pulsing phenomenon in the doorway. The best – or perhaps worst – was now to come, as, when I was calling out for phenomena, something pulled the clipboard in my hand! I was quite surprised, to say the least, because this was something physical. I turned on my torch and looked around; the other team members were about 3ft away.

Somewhat reluctantly, I turned off my torch and asked the spirit in the room to do this again – and lo and behold, it felt as though someone tried to pull the damn thing out of my hand! It was tugged so hard that my arm was pulled forward. I shone the torch yet again, and when I realised no one was near me I knew there and then we had had a result. This was the end of the vigil at this location, and what an investigation!

Never before investigated, and unlikely to be investigated again, the Coroner's Court, in our opinion, had – and perhaps still has – an entity or spirit that roamed the whole premises causing mischief and generally letting people know it resides there. There was nothing untoward or malevolent about it, and we think it is that of a male.

A lock-off video camera.

The similarities between the reported phenomena of the investigation vigils were very striking. Both units heard the guttural breath or laugh, and both units witnessed the pulsing phenomenon too. We all witnessed a physical experience – my clipboard being tugged twice, and Drew's left arm being grabbed.

To think that we were intending to investigate the neighbouring nightclub after it closed to the public. It turns out that what we had hoped to do, we did not. Instead, we ended up doing something all night we did not expect to. The phrase 'expect the unexpected' springs to mind!

The El Coto Restaurant – City Centre

The El Coto Spanish restaurant is situated in the centre of Newcastle upon Tyne on Leazes Park Road and stands opposite the magnificent 1880 John Johnson's synagogue. It is thought that David Stephenson designed Leazes Park Road in around 1811, and it was originally named Albion Place, the continuation of Albion Street. It is believed that between 1896 and 1914 the name was changed to Leazes Park Road. Number 21 Leazes Park Road, the site of the El Coto restaurant, has a rich and varied history dating back to at least 1811 with a whole host of people having worked and lived at this location.

The El Coto restaurant on Leazes Park Road.

The long corridor where our motion sensors were tripped by an unseen presence.

Although the area is called Gallowgate, the Newcastle gallows were situated elsewhere (on the site of the BBC television and radio studios on Barrack Road). However, it is rumoured that hangings did indeed take place on the site of this restaurant, specifically in the adjacent courtyard. One hanging is believed to have taken place in the front of the building. Over the years the property has seen many faces come and go, from grocers, insurance agents, cabinetmakers, joiners and sofa manufacturers to a gunsmith and a solicitor – to name but a few. It has been used as a private dwelling, for trade and commerce, and is now currently a thriving city-centre restaurant.

I think 21 Leazes Park Road has seen it all. It is not surprising that the area – and this particular property – is reputed to be haunted by a number of ghosts and spirits. Lost souls wondering aimlessly around the property in search of peace? Or ghosts who once resided here and liked the place so much they did not want to depart? This is what the owners and staff of El Coto have been asking themselves after a series of inexplicable happenings.

Dark figures have been seen moving about the place, mysterious knocking is heard coming from the passage windows when no one is around, footsteps in empty rooms are often heard and, more chillingly, it was reported that a member of staff who ventured upstairs on his own to the upper restaurant sensed he was being followed.

He stopped in his tracks and then heard a voice directly behind him; when he turned around, no one was there. He was the only person in that wing of the building at this particular time, and by all accounts he was terrified.

So who or what is causing the disturbances? The North East Ghost Research Team was called in to investigate after the owner contacted me. Fascinated by the ghostly goings-on, the owner and staff alike wanted some answers.

On the night of Sunday 22 January 2006, the team turned up at the property to conduct an all-night investigation. Tony Liddell, (author of the book *Otherworld North East, Ghosts and Hauntings Explored*), and one or two guest investigators joined us. We started the evening with a tour of the premises before splitting into two groups to cover the location. The first location for investigation was the upper-floor restaurant. We ventured in and began investigations at 11.15 p.m. A preliminary baseline test of the room showed no anomalous readings, so we waited and observed. The room temperature was 23 degrees and, although it was a January night, the humidity levels were quite high. This particular vigil proved to be a rich source of minor paranormal activity as one or two disembodied breaths were heard by a few of those present. I also thought I saw a black shadow move across the floor from left to right. We were all stationary at this time.

Our team psychic, Suzanne also picked up on a hanging and specified it was related to the building itself and not the area in which we were. The other group at this time was down in the restaurant cellars, but they had a slow start to the evening with only a few taps and knocks heard which, I dare say, could have been the building settling down for the night. Our other team psychic, Glenn Hall, did, however, pick up on a chubby, grey-haired fellow with a moustache, and said he had a blue apron on. He was given the name Dolan. Could he have been a joiner, or one of the many tradesmen that are known to have worked there?

We regrouped at 12.15 a.m. and had a quick break before heading off to our subsequent locations. It was our turn in the cellars, and it did not disappoint. We were only sitting in the cellar for about a minute or so when I felt a sharp pull on the bottom of my right trouser leg; this was accompanied by a sharp drop in temperature, which adds credibility to the occurrence. The temperature in the room then returned to its original reading of 23 degrees. Our team psychic Suzanne then complained of feeling dizzy and disorientated and said she couldn't – or wouldn't – turn her back on the doorway, for reasons she could not specify. She also picked up on a spirit person called Headley, but could not determine if it was a man or woman. Interestingly enough, census records do show that in 1881 a family resided at this residence with a boarder or lodger named Heddon. Could this have been the person Suzanne meant? After all, messages do indeed come through somewhat jumbled and unclear at times. The ambient room temperature at this point then dropped again.

The most interesting results in the cellar were yet to come. While we were calling out to the atmosphere, it was noted by team investigator Darren Olley that a plastic bag hanging up in the cellar was rustling. When he looked to see what the noise was, he noticed it was swaying slightly from side to side although there was no one near it at the time. Draughts and breezes were eliminated in our initial baseline recordings.

The lower restaurant area of the complex.

A mist anomaly was then seen in the middle of the room by guest investigator Tony Liddell (visible to the naked eye). It was accompanied by a massive drop in both temperature and humidity, but unfortunately the night-vision video cameras we had running at the time failed to record any hard evidence of this mist. This annoyed us all no end, but that is how ghost hunting is. Nevertheless, this was a fascinating vigil which produced some compelling results.

Onwards to the next location, the entrance foyer and reception area to the restaurant. This vigil proved very quiet indeed in regards to actual, auditory phenomena, but the coffee machine and the credit-card machine did seem to turn on for no reason and begin functioning. We thought this was odd, but the restaurant staff that joined us on the investigation told us this was quite normal and a rational explanation was found. However, two interesting photographs were taken in this vigil. Both of these photographs were taken by two different investigators using different cameras at different times in the vigil. The anomalies both appear in the same area of the room, showing a similar streak of anomalous light. What they are for sure is still baffling investigators and they are the cause of much debate within the paranormal research field. At present they are believed to be orbs in movement, or spirit paths or doorways into our world called vortices. Until more research is done on these types of phenomena we can't say exactly what they are, although hairs and clothing fibres are another possibility!

Our last location in the investigation was the downstairs restaurant area. Suzanne almost straight away picked up on a spirit lady called Cynthia Labelle or Label, but research showed no one of that name having worked or resided at this property.

Filming the trigger objects.

Knocks, taps, and what we all thought were footsteps were heard in abundance during this vigil; a dictation machine was also moved across the top of the counter by an unseen hand. This seems to have occurred while we were all sitting at the opposite end of the room, observing and monitoring the area. It's interesting to note we all heard shuffling and movement coming from the area in which the dictation machine was placed. When we went over to take a look, we found the sound-recording device had been moved quite a distance from where it was left. A good result. My night-vision video camera was then trained upon the dictation machine in the hope it would move again on tape, but alas, it did not.

Whilst monitoring this location we left our infra-red beam barriers down in the corridor hoping something might trip the beam. I ventured to the top of the downstairs restaurant to take a look down the corridor and, in retrospect; it was probably the best thing I had done that night. As I looked down the corridor I saw one of our guest investigators, standing at least 5 or 6ft away from the sensors, taking photographs. Suddenly, the motion sensor was tripped and the alarms went off. This gave the guest investigator a bit of a fright, and he exited the corridor quite quickly! No one was near the sensors when they went off, as I, the guest investigator and another team member can verify. The sensors were left for the rest of the investigation and failed to go off again. In addition to that, they were also checked after the investigation, and it has been determined that the batteries were indeed working soundly. So, who tripped the beam?

It is also very interesting to note that Tony Liddell was monitoring the area at the time from the downstairs restaurant and, as before in the cellars, a magnificent temperature drop accompanied this phenomenon. It was also one of the areas that the owner had told us was very active, with strange phenomena reported by the staff.

To summarise, the investigation carried out at the El Coto restaurant on 22 January 2006 was a fascinating one. Although the investigation was rather slow to begin with, paranormal phenomena did indeed occur and were witnessed and recorded by the majority of investigators attending. Although different types of phenomena were witnessed at different times during the night, fortunately more than one person witnessed them at the same time. This fact alone makes the phenomena all the more credible. It is not often that this happens on investigations, as usually there is only one who bears witness to any alleged phenomena and, as is often the case, they question themselves as to whether it actually happened at all. For this reason the investigation at El Coto is one I will always remember. The evidence accrued is, I believe, very credible and helps to support the theory and the validity of ghosts and hauntings.

The building itself, as mentioned earlier, dates back to the middle 1800s and has seen a lot of people come and go. Remember, when ghost hunters investigate buildings and properties, nine times out of ten it is the actual shell and fabric of the building that is being investigated, and not the modern-day interior that it houses (in this case a Spanish restaurant).

The eerie corridor where strange noises have been heard – by both residents and investigators.

'Tom' of the Bigg Market

Mentioned earlier in the book is an account of a haunted flat in the Bigg Market area of the city. If the reader recalls, some very strange activity had been reported at this particular household and the girls living there were quite ambivalent about it.

On the night of 14 June 2008, G.H.O.S.T. arrived at the Bigg Market on one of the busiest nights you could imagine to carry out a full investigation of the flat. Mark Winter and I arrived at about 10.30 p.m. and were soon met by Drew, Fiona, and brothers Jim and Paul Collins. Two other team members, Lloyd Wright and Lee Stephenson, were unavailable for this investigation. At 10.50 p.m., Fiona and Paul carried out the initial baseline tests in the apartment and discovered no anomalies whatsoever. Squeaky floorboards were discovered in certain areas of the flat, draughts and winds from outside were virtually non-existent and the average room temperature was between 20-22 degrees. An array of trigger objects was placed down in respective locations and motion sensors and beam barriers were situated in the upper and lower corridors. Finally, both the CCTV and laptop were set up and we were ready to begin.

It must be noted that after the baselines had been carried out – and before the first vigil had begun – the ghostly presences were already beginning to make themselves known. A large white light was seen to appear at one end of the upper corridor and it moved towards Drew with speed. It shot over his shoulder as he ducked to miss it. Not long after this incident it was reported by Drew, Fiona, Jim and Paul that the toilet door handle had been moved up and down. No rational cause was found. We then split up into three groups at first to cover the flat. Group one was Fiona, Gemma Gorner, and her two friends, Rebecca and Karen; they investigated the upper corridors. Group two comprised of Drew, Mark and Jim; they investigated the entrance hall and corridor. Paul and I investigated the living room.

During our first vigil in the living room we called out to the atmosphere to see if anything would occur, but to no avail. I then tried some electronic voice phenomena (EVP) experiments, but these yielded no results either. The only odd occurrence during this stint was when I was filming with my video camera and it turned itself off in my hands. Why it did this, I don't know. Drew, Mark and Jim, when investigating the entrance foyer, experienced an oddity when they found that the previously locked toilet door had been opened. Again, no explanation was forthcoming as to how this may have happened. Upstairs, the girls experienced phenomena that would end up repeating themselves later in the investigation. Gemma and Karen heard the sound of someone whistling – the sound was coming from inside their location.

During our first break, Gemma's flatmate Liz Mills returned home and joined the investigation. The groups re-situated themselves in new locations, but they didn't stay in them for long. Things took a bizarre turn when Drew, Mark and Jim were investigating the upper corridor. Paul and I were investigating the entrance hall and corridor at the time and we could clearly hear the team upstairs. Our vigils were interrupted when we heard Drew call out and ask if the alleged spirit would make itself known. A clear and distinct whistle was heard by all upstairs and also by the team downstairs. I actually called out to Drew and asked if the whistle came from any of the investigators, and was told it did not.

Upon asking for more phenomena, we heard knocking down in the entrance foyer, which was rather odd to say the least, and then suddenly a tremendous series of crashes and bumps were heard coming from the upper corridor.

'Did you hear that?' Drew called out.

'Yes I did – what the hell was it?' I bellowed up the stairs.

'I don't know yet, I am checking it out', replied Drew.

Suddenly, from out of the darkness came a number of choice words that I dare not mention here. As it turned out, the cross trigger object had launched itself from its position (which was on the floor at the end of the corridor) and travelled about 4ft across the floor, landing just short of the motion sensors. By this time, Paul and I had run upstairs to see what was going on and saw the object lying *in situ*. Jim hurried past us along the corridor in absolute terror; he was getting out of there! Drew rewound the video camera footage and we all watched it. The noise is clearly heard as the three investigators stand at the opposite end of the corridor to where the object was placed; on the footage, one can see Jim and Mark – both down the corridor at the time with Drew, who was filming there. No one was near the trigger object when it was launched with force down the corridor.

After hearing thumps and bangs for a few seconds this trigger object was found by the investigators after it had been displaced. As you can see it wasn't just moved slightly – it must have been thrown.

We then reconvened downstairs and met up with the girls. They had known something was going on as they too heard the object as it was moved but decided to stay in their respective vigil location. Cups of tea and coffee were drunk while the investigators excitedly discussed what had just happened. I then decided to return to the corridor in question with my EVP recorder and carry out some tests. Mark, Fiona, and flatmate Liz Mills accompanied me. I proceeded to switch on the device and began recording. I asked a number of questions, leaving enough time for any residing spirit to reply with – we were not disappointed. After posing about ten questions or so we were rewarded with replies to two of the questions.

One question was, 'How old are you?' A distant voice can be heard clearly saying afterwards, 'forty-eight'. The other question was, 'Do you know that you are dead?' The same voice said 'yes'. Spine-chilling results! The EVP recording was immediately downloaded onto the laptop and analysed. The rest of the night was spent discussing the paranormal events that had taken place until a séance was held in the area where the activity had taken place. The séance lasted over forty-five minutes. During the proceedings I was pushed by something in the darkness. It knocked me back a little and it didn't feel as though it was friendly. Minor temperature drops and the occasional breeze were also felt by some of the circle members and then the activity seemed to dry up.

This investigation proved to be a very good night for all concerned, with some brilliant activity documented and witnessed. The girls for some time now had been reporting very similar occurrences at their Newcastle home, and were now convinced they were not imagining all of it. Our investigation there verified the fact that something uncanny was happening which warranted further investigation. A second investigation will be undertaken there in the future, in the hope that we can gather more evidence of the haunting – and who knows, maybe next time we might just catch the ghost himself on tape.

AFTERWORD

I was raised in the Walker area of Newcastle upon Tyne which is now known as River's Gate, and as a child my father often told me tales of the local spectres, ghosts, wraiths, or whatever you wish to call them, that haunted Newcastle upon Tyne. From that point on I had a fascination with the paranormal forever growing inside me and, after experiencing a few odd occurrences in my 'old family home', I decided to try to learn more about them. Before we go any further, let me tell you about my earliest recollection of what I deemed to be 'paranormal activity'.

It was when I was about the age of ten. The strange occurrences always began when I was sent to bed and when I was the only one in the house upstairs. Since my brother Gary was three years older than I, he was allowed to stay up later. As I lay in bed trying to get to sleep with the landing light left on, I often heard the sound of the stairs creaking as if someone was creeping slowly up them. Most people would say that houses creak and groan at night, and of course I agree; however, the difference in this case was that it seemed like every creak or noise the stair made during these episodes coincided with what noises would have been made if somebody had been actually ascending the staircase. Some stairs made recognisable and distinguishing noises and other stairs did not make any noise at all.

Ultimately I became convinced that someone or something was creeping up the stairs. As I lay there, frozen solid in my bed, the noises on the stairs increasingly became louder as though whoever or whatever was making its ascent was getting closer to my room. The creaks and bumps kept on coming as I became more terrified until they reached what sounded like the top of the stairs. I hoped it might have been my mother or father checking up on me to make sure I was asleep, but on calling out to them I had no response which frightened me even more. I soon began to realise that whoever or whatever was present was now standing behind my bedroom door. It always seemed to stop there every time this happened. Then, as I was lying there in total silence under the blankets, gripped with absolute fear, the breathing began! I could hear the distinctive and clear noise of slow breathing from behind the door. At this point I could take no more and would literally scream for my parents. I would

Newcastle Quayside pre-1771. (Courtesy of Newcastle Libraries and Information Service)

hear the downstairs door open, and can remember hearing the voices of my father, mother and brother at the bottom of the stairs in the living room, which clearly indicates to me that it could not have been a family member creeping about. This happened on countless occasions and I am convinced I heard what I heard. I was wide awake and I was 100 per cent positive I did not imagine any of it. I can still remember those noises like it was yesterday, and although admittedly it scared me half to death I was seriously intrigued and I wanted to learn and experience more.

Buying books and magazines on the subject was a good start. From there I learned about all the famous hauntings – Borley Rectory, the Enfield Poltergeist – along with the theories and ideas that were put forward to try and explain them; I found it all most intriguing. Since then, my interest and enthusiasm for the subject has grown (as well as my book and literature collection) and has developed into something that I consider a passion, a way of life, and not just a passing fad or a hobby. Please understand I feel hobbies and pastimes are admirable and anyone that takes an interest in the paranormal has my vote, but for me I think it was always more than that – and where better to take an active interest in the paranormal than in my home town?

In comparison to cities as such York, Edinburgh, Derby and London – the cities known world-wide for their vast array of ghost tales and legends – Newcastle was, until fairly recently, more or less virgin territory and untouched by paranormal investigators and psychical researchers. Why, I don't know: I feel Newcastle had most certainly been habitually overlooked in regards to its resident ghosts, but nowadays, with the fascination with the paranormal at a new high due to television programmes such as

Most Haunted and *Ghost Hunters*, things are different. Many groups of investigators and aficionados of the paranormal are now heading off into the night in venues all over the world in search of evidence to prove the existence of the denizens of the otherworld. I am no different.

You could say that it has been a labour of love researching this book, and bringing together the wonderful ghost tales and legends that are associated with Newcastle, our beautiful and remarkable city. Visiting the venues featured herein and listening to so many wonderful people from all walks of life as they speak of their strange but fascinating accounts of a world that lies just beyond our own senses really does make my job as a writer and a paranormal investigator all the more enjoyable.

To visit old public houses and to hear all about their spectres while supping a pint of the landlord's finest is not work – it's a pleasure. Likewise, being shown around historic properties by their respective wardens or custodians is also a very delightful and educational experience. As I learn the histories and soak up the ambience of wherever I may be, I attempt to reach far back in time and metaphorically touch what was once here many, many years ago, at the same time hoping, just hoping that the resident ghost decides to make an appearance during my visit. Personally speaking, this is ghost hunting at its best.

I suppose when I reflect on what I do (which is quite often) I question myself and contemplate why this line of work is 'a labour of love'. It's a funny phrase, isn't it? I mean … who enjoys work? Love, however, it most certainly is. Labour, the labour – if you can call it that – actually begins back at home when I begin to write about my adventures. Having said that, sitting at my PC mulling over the day's events, with my fingers giving it 'fifty to the dozen', is almost as enjoyable as the actual field research itself. Playing back my pre-recorded interviews, trying not to miss one iota of detail while documenting my findings, can be quite therapeutic and extremely satisfying. Don't get me wrong, I am not saying that there is no work involved in ghost hunting – on the contrary, it can be very hard work – but because the work I do is such an immense pleasure for me it does not feel like it.

As I sit here in my office at home writing these words, I look back on what has been achieved, and take great delight in the fact that, up to this point in my life, a lot of my hard work is now in print and people from all over the North East of England and beyond may very well own copies of my books and read about my activities. If I have raised a single eyebrow, perhaps made one person stop and think, or even given someone the incentive to do some ghost hunting of their own, it has all been worthwhile.

Being born and bred in Tyneside, it was an honour and privilege to be allowed to compile such a book on the history and haunts of Newcastle's folk. I feel rather fortunate to have had the opportunity to write this book about a subject so close to my heart in regards to a city that is even closer. I hope you, the reader, have enjoyed meandering through these pages of fabulous ghost tales and strange accounts as much as I have enjoyed investigating them and writing them up.

BIBLIOGRAPHY & RECOMMENDED READING

Armstrong, Pamela, *Dark Tales of Old Newcastle* (Bridge Studios, 1990)
Charleton, *History of Newcastle upon Tyne* (Harold Hill & Son, 1950)
Day, James Wentworth, *In Search of Ghosts* (Muller, 1969)
Graham, Frank, *Historic Newcastle* (Frank Graham, 1970)
Graham Frank, *Newcastle* (Frank Graham, 1978)
Hallowell, Michael J., *Mystery Animals of Northumberland and Tyneside* (CFZ, 2008)
Hallum, Jack, *Ghosts of the North* (David & Charles, 1976)
Haining, Peter, *Ghosts* (BCA, 1974)
Hapgood, Sarah, *500 British Ghosts and Hauntings* (Foulsham, 1993)
Harper, Charles G., *Haunted Houses* (Senate, 1907)
Harries, John, *The Ghost Hunters Road Book* (Letts, 1968)
Histon, Vanessa, *Ghosts of Grainger Town* (Tyne Bridge Publishing, 2001)
Hippisley Coxe, Antony A., *Haunted Britain* (Pan, 1973)
Hurwitz, Stanley, *The Great Fire of Gateshead and Newcastle* (Stanley Hurwitz, 1971)
MacKenzie, Andrew, *Hauntings and Apparitions* (Heinemann, 1982)
Maple, Eric, *Supernatural England* (Hale, 1977)
Norman, Diana, *The Stately Ghosts of England* (Muller, 1963)
O' Donnell, Elliot, *Haunted Britain* (Rider, 1948)
Poole, Keith B., *Haunted Heritage* (Guild Publishing, 1988)
Price, Harry, *Poltergeist over England* (Country Life Ltd, 1945)
Ritson, Darren W., *Ghost Hunter, True Life Encounters from the North East* (GHP, 2006)
Ritson, Darren W., *In Search of Ghosts, Real Hauntings from Around Britain* (GHP, 2007)
Underwood, Peter, *This Haunted Isle* (Harrap, 1984)
Underwood, Peter, *A Gazetteer of British Ghosts* (Souvenir Press, 1971)
Underwood, Peter, *A-Z of British Ghosts* (Souvenir Press, 1971)